Living with Neurofibromatosis

By

Kirsty Ashton M.B.E

With lots of love
Kirsty Ashton
x

Published by New Generation Publishing in 2014

Copyright © Kirsty Ashton 2014

First Edition

The author asserts the moral right under the Copyright, Designs and Patents Act 1988 to be identified as the author of this work.

All Rights reserved. No part of this publication may be reproduced, stored in a retrieval system or transmitted, in any form or by any means without the prior consent of the author, nor be otherwise circulated in any form of binding or cover other than that which it is published and without a similar condition being imposed on the subsequent purchaser.

www.newgeneration-publishing.com

New Generation Publishing

According to the feedback I received from my first book, no one kept to the rules of not crying.

So this time the only rule I am going to give is that the tears that you may shed are tears of happiness and not sadness.

As myself and other people share our NF stories with you, remember we are doing this to bring awareness of the condition and to help make NF a household name in the hope that one day we will have found a cure for this cruel condition.

If you read my first book, you will know that my life is quite eventful at times, so this is a follow-up to tell you everything that's been happening to me since my first book (*Kirsty's story living with Neurofibromatosis and scoliosis*). For those who haven't read my first book, don't worry, I will give you a short version of my story, or you can still buy a copy of my first book.

With love from

Kirsty x x x

Preface

Kirsty
Life is a pool of water – sometimes muddy, sometimes iced over and sometimes warm and clear with sunshine dancing on the surface. People enter your world and cause ripples in the water – some people who are on the edge of the pond will cause an occasional ripple with a Christmas card or a Facebook poke.

Others, more to the centre, are the people you went to school with, worked with 'back in the day', all a little bit heavier and a little greyer: 'You've not changed one bit' we lie.
   And, in the very centre of the pond, is your family, the ones who have given you life, and the ones in turn you've given life to.

So far so normal and straightforward, until the time a stone is unexpectedly lobbed into the pond and the ripples wash across everyone, rocking a little tide up against the banks making passers' by stop and look – you, yes you! reading this right now – you're one of the passers' by, attention momentarily pulled by this book, your path through this shop, past this shelf or wherever this book lay – you were passing by but something caught you – ripples lapping the bank as the pond recovers from a beautiful, seemingly slight yet incredibly powerful stone dropping into the pond. That stone is Kirsty. Once met she's never forgotten… a beautiful young lady with a heart of gold who lands in your life and makes an impact not only on you but on everyone else around you.

I met Kirsty through my wife Julie Hesmondhalgh who played Hayley Cropper in Coronation Street: she meets a lot of people in her work does Julie, and I, as a writer in the cellar of our house meet far fewer people than her. She'd tell me about one or two people she'd met, how their stories impacted on her and how she'd like to help them – whether it be providing an autographed *Rover's Return* beermat for them to auction off, opening an event, selling raffle tickets, sponsoring their charity bike-ride, attending a fundraiser ball etc. Very, very rarely does one of the people she meet become part of our lives – Kirsty did, and is very much part of our life.

Kirsty was like any other girl (when we met her) and (now) woman her age – she's bright as a button and as daft as a brush; she makes you laugh, she makes you think, she's got energy, enthusiasm, essentially – she's got life! This book continues her journey from her previous book (also available but not necessary to have read before reading this – a bit like watching *Toy Story 2* - you don't need to have seen the first one but it helps) and charts the next phase in Kirsty's life – going from a poorly child to a woman with an on-going medical condition that will not stop her from doing anything else in life a woman of her age wants to do. She's brave, she's fearless and what you'll read in the following pages will make you LOL, ROFL and break your heart! Just as Kirsty has dropped into the centre of your life, your pond, the ripples of this book will wash over everyone you know as you share Kirsty's story and learn from it that life is for living, it's not about that extra hour in bed and slobbing in front of the television (although that's nice every now and again!), it's about seizing it and running with it, kicking and screaming and laughing and crying and living to the full. Kirsty lives life to the full! Come on in, the water's lovely!

By: Ian Kershaw

A special "Thank you" to the following people who have helped in putting this book together

Preface
Mr Ian Kershaw

Front cover design
Mr Mike Lee

Publisher
Mr Daniel Cooke
(New Generation Publishing)
Sam Rennie
(New Generation Publishing, My adviser)
Mandy Tragner
(New Generation Publishing Proof-reader)

Contents

Preface 4
Introduction 8
About My Family and Me 9
Short version of my story from my previous book 14
My NF Journey Continues 17
Stories from other People who have NF 80
What is Neurofibromatosis? 194
Some pictures showing signs of NF 204
Neurofibromatosis Question and Answers 210
Useful NF1 Links 221
What some of my doctors have to say 223
What some of my friends have to say 239
Some Fun Times 246
Charities that I support 288
My Supporters 295
My Goals in Life 298
Glossary 300
Acknowledgements 314
Some reviews from my first book: 316

Introduction

When Kirsty was 11 weeks old she was diagnosed with Neurofibromatosis (NF1), which caused no problems until she was eight years old when she was also diagnosed with scoliosis. She now lives a very different, but full life, where her family and a large group of friends surround her, some of who have made a contribution to this book with their own thoughts.

In 1998 Kirsty was enjoying weekly swimming lessons, she had joined a dance school and enjoyed dancing on stage and putting on shows for charity. Fifteen years on and Kirsty can no longer dance or swim as well as she could when she was eight years old. She had to give it all up due to being in so much pain.

An operation at The Royal Manchester Children's Hospital in March 2005 to place two titanium rods on either side of Kirsty's spine came with risk. Eight hours into the twelve-hour operation the surgeon had to stop due to complications. The surgeon needed to ask for further advice on what to do next and said he had never before seen so many tumours on anyone's spine.

Kirsty's story tells how and why her life changed due to the problems caused by Neurofibromatosis and Scoliosis.

Perhaps the most remarkable thing about Kirsty is her attitude. Kirsty loves to laugh and joke around, and unless you are among her closest friends and family, you would probably never know she was suffering with so much pain. Kirsty is an unbelievable young woman, and I challenge anyone to deal with this crippling situation with a better attitude than Kirsty does.

About My Family and Me

My Brother (Chris), Dad (John), Me and Mum (Julie)

I was born on the 5th April 1990 in Wythenshawe Hospital, Manchester, weighing in at 6lb 13oz. My big brother, Christopher picked my name (Kirsty). I have a nickname which all my close friends call me, which is "Kay", and my other nickname is — "Titch" as I am the smallest one of all my friends.

I'm told I was a happy baby and always blowing bubbles with my mouth. Soon after I was born, Mum noticed some brown marks on my skin (café-au-lait marks) and mentioned them to the pediatric doctor when he did his ward round; the doctor dismissed the marks saying it was nothing to worry about. But my mum knew different and at 11 weeks old I was diagnosed with Neurofibromatosis (NF1). My mum also has this condition so it came as no surprise to her.

When I was about eight month old I was modeling for Tuesday's Child and did some catalogue work. Mum said everyone loved me because I could whistle by the age of 11 months and I was also out of nappies by the time I was a year old, and every time the cameraman went to take a picture I would hold myself and shout "POT", which meant I needed the potty.

I started walking just before my first birthday and I was pretty much on target with all my health checks that babies have. The only thing I had to do was visit the hospital every six months to keep an eye on my NF for any problems that could crop up.

I was fine up until the age of eight; I enjoyed swimming, dance and gym classes, I had even managed to complete my gold badge and swim a mile before I was nine years old.

My favourite colour is blue and I'm not really a girly girl; I love my jeans and tops, I feel much more relaxed in casual clothes.

I don't let my disabilities get me down. I enjoy raising money for other poorly children who have different illness not just Neurofibromatosis; I work very closely with the charities "When You Wish Upon a Star" and "Children with Tumours". I raise X amount of money for the poorly children and pass it over to the charities so they are able to use the money raised.

I joined Peel Hall Primary School in the September of 1995, where I stayed until I moved on to Altrincham College of Arts in the September of 2001. Although I missed almost a year of schooling in Year ten, I still managed to pass 15 G.C.S.E's /G.N.V.Q's; nine of them being A-C grade. My English teacher said I was mild dyslexic and helped me all he could. When I came out of hospital after a three-month stay I had lessons at home 3 hours a week.

I attended Trafford college for three years where I studded a range of subjects. I went on to university to do a Foundation Degree in Radio Production and NVQ in Business and Administration. I also did my CACHE Level 2 Certificate in Supporting Teaching and Learning in Schools. Since leaving university I applied to the BBC, which supports disabled people called "extend". My role was a production team assistant in children's.

I have been lucky enough to stay within the BBC since this scheme and I am now in Learning as a production Management assistant.

Extend scheme what is it?

If you have a disability recognised by the Equality Act 2010 and you are successful upon application, you will be given six months. There is no guarantee you will get a job after the six months, but it gives you the skills and training in which you need to help you.

I live at home with my mum, dad and brother Chris, but hope to get my own house one day.

I hope you enjoy reading my diary that I have shared with you; so many people who read my first book kept asking if I would write an update on my journey with NF, which is why I have written this second book.

I don't know what the future holds for me, but whatever happens I'm sure it will be interesting. You can keep up with all my news by visiting my website at www.kirstysstory.co.uk, and if you can help with my fundraising for "When You Wish Upon a Star" or 'Children with Tumours', please visit my justgiving links on my website. —Thank You.

The information I have given in this book should **NOT be considered to be medical advice**. It is not meant to replace the advice of the physician who cares for you or your child.

My Mum, Julie

My mum and I are very close. She has always been there for me and tends not to let things bother her, unless Chris or I are ill that is. We have the same sense of humour and we have been known to borrow each other's clothes and shoes.

Mum stayed with me all the time I was in hospital and even slept on a chair next to my bed for two months. I often kid people and say my mum is my big sister: well, she is young looking for her age.

My mum also suffers from Neurofibromatosis NF1; mum was not diagnosed until the age of ten years. My mum found a small lump on the side of her tummy and told her mum about it after visiting the doctors my mum was sent to the hospital for more tests at which time she was diagnosed with NF1. My mum gets very upset that she passed the condition on to me and it upsets me to see my mum getting so upset. I don't blame my mum; I could still have been born with the condition even if my mum did not have NF.

My Dad, John

My dad and I are very different and don't always see eye to eye. But he's always there for me, I love him and he is a great dad.

My dad was unable to stay in hospital due to work commitments but came to see me almost every day. My dad works nights and the hospital was a good drive away from our home.

My dad works hard to provide for our family so is not able to attend my hospital visits with me, but he always asks how I have got on and wants to know what the doctors have said. My dad often acts as my taxicab too.

My Brother, Christopher

Chris is three and half years older than me. We only argue over silly things really, like who's had the last can of coke and who is better looking, which we both know is me, or something really silly and unimportant. He's always looked out for me and is a protective big brother. He also gives the best hugs.

My brother would turn up at the hospital after work, sometimes this would be as late as 10pm, the nurses etc., would still let him in as they knew how much it meant to me to see my brother and we never made any noise – well, we tried not to.

I hope my brother knows how much I love him, and knows I'll always be there for him too. My brother will be moving out of the family home soon and the only thing that I am looking forward to is having his bedroom.

Short version of my story from my previous book

I was born with a condition called Neurofibromatosis (NF1). The condition gave me no real problems until I was eight years old, at which time I was diagnosed with scoliosis. I had numerous scans and x-rays to find the cause of my scoliosis, the results of these test showed that I had lots of tumours on my spine.

I saw enough doctors to more than fill my notes with correspondence. The neurofibromatosis had caused my spine to curve to one side. The doctor I was seeing at the time wanted me to wear a Boston back brace (a hard plastic jacket), 24 hours a day; seven days a week. I had no real issues wearing the back brace and I wore it for the next six years.

At the age of 14 my spine started to worsen; the brace was doing nothing for me, so on the 9th March 2005 I went into hospital under the care of Mr Neil Oxborrow (the best spinal doctor in the UK).

During my spinal surgery my spinal cord was monitored to make sure that it carried on working correctly during the surgery.

Any type of surgery on the spine carries a small risk that the spinal cord doesn't like what the doctors are doing. Halfway through my operation the monitoring started to suggest my spinal cord was not happy. I was woken up and I remember being asked to move my toes, I could not move them at first and doctors were worried that some damage had been caused to my spine. Back on HDU I continued to be very poorly, and was told I had to have more surgery as only half of the spinal surgery had been done. It was the 25th March 2005 before I was well enough to have such a big operation. This time everything went without any cause for concern.

Back on the HDU I started vomiting, which got so bad over the following weeks that I lost over two stone in weight. I ended up being in hospital for over three months.

As the years have past, my NF1 has caused me many problems. My neurofibromas are growing mainly internally and not on the skin (although I do have some on the skin), I have been told by doctors that I have tumours on most of the nerves as they leave my spine and on many of the big nerves in my arms and legs. There is no way these tumours can all be removed without causing major nerve damage and so my NF doctor carefully monitors me.

Some of the tumours are beginning to cause my nerves not to work properly, I have developed weak ankles with foot drop and my knees keep giving way.

I have also developed a condition called Gastroparisis, which means that I cannot keep any fluid down and I get very dehydrated, and have spent weeks in hospital at a time when the sickness has been really bad.

I love helping people and being around others. When I was nine years old I had a wish granted by the "When You Wish Upon a Star" charity, – my brother had wrote to them telling them all about me and that I wanted to visit Santa in Lapland – I received a call to say my wish was going to be granted. On this magical trip I met another young girl who had cancer, we became really good friends telling each other what we wanted to do when we got older and just having a good giggle. When we got back to the airport we exchanged phone number and address, gave each other a really big hug and said we would see each other very soon. Less than two weeks later my mum received a call from the mum of my new friend saying that sadly her daughter had passed away. I was so upset by this news (I was only nine) I just did not understand why it had to happen to such a lovely person.

I asked my mum about the wish we had both been on to visit Santa in Lapland, my mum explained that if the money had not been raised that we would not have been given our wish to see Santa. From hearing my mum say this I decided I wanted to make sure that other brave and poorly children went on the same magical trip that my friend and I went on, and in 2008 I had raised enough money to send 100 poorly children on a trip to visit Santa in Lapland.

My fundraising continues, and I have received many awards in recognition for the fundraising that I do. I have met many celebrities; some who still continue to support me and who are there for me when I need them most.

If you want to read my full story you will have to buy a copy of the book (*Kirsty's Story Living with Neurofibromatosis and Scoliosis*) – the royalties from which are going to a children's charity.

My NF Journey Continues

This is where my book picks up from; you will read what has happened to me since my last book.

I am always being asked how I do I cope, but I really don't see any other way but to cope. I believe in making the most out of what life has given me. I enjoy helping people and I can't change the past but I can make what lies ahead for my future go the way I want it to. I can be very stubborn and I am as daft as a brush (my mum and dad will agree), I think being stubborn helps. I will not let my health stop me from enjoying life and I will not let anything get the better of me.

In this new book, as well as updating you on my life story, I have included some stories from other people who suffer from NF. I decided to include other NF stories as NF effects everyone differently. I hope by including other stories it will help you in some way understand more about NF and how it can affect people so differently.

Here we go with my follow-up.

3rd March 2010:
I went to see Dr Watts over my constant sickness (I suffer from Gastroparisis), she now wants me to start taking Domparidon three times a day alongside what I am already taking. Not sure it will have any effect, as I tried this medication when I was in hospital for four weeks last year and it did not help then. I mentioned that I knew someone that does hypnotherapy and that I was thinking of giving it a go.

Hypnosis is thought to work by altering our state of consciousness in a way that the left side of our brain is turned off, while the right side is made more alert. For example, someone who consciously wants to overcome their fear of spiders may try everything they consciously can to do it, but will still fail as long as their subconscious mind retains this terror and prevents them from succeeding.

I am willing to give hypnosis a go, in the hope it will stop me from being sick all the time. Dr Watts is going to refer me to the hospital hypnotherapist, but in the meantime I am letting one of my relatives, who is a qualified hypnotherapist, try and cure me.

I have also had one of three swabs done to see if I am still carrying the MRSA bug and should get the results next week.

18th March 2010:
I have had a bad few days with the sickness and had to be admitted to hospital to have some fluid via a drip and anti- sickness injections given at the hospital, I have also been given some more anti-sickness tablets in the hope it will settle the sickness down.

14th April 2010:
I had a really nice week away with my mum, but the sickness was still the same and I kept being sick on the plane. Mum just asked the steward for a few extra sick bags.

When I got back home I had a few hospital letters waiting for me. Dr Watts had been told about my recent trip to A&E due to the sickness and she's asked to see me again next week. I was not meant to be seeing her again until August so I am not sure why she wants to see me so early really.

I have also got to see the anaesthetist on the 20th April so he can have chat over the operation that I am having on my knees.

Over the next few weeks I have got my hydrotherapy, E.N.T for my ears, hypnotherapy (to see if it will help with the sickness) and the pain clinic.

I have still not heard back from Mr Neil Oxborrow about my spine, but I have been in so much pain with my back and I have worn my back brace a lot more over the past few weeks.

29th April 2010:
I went to hospital this week to see the doctor about my continued sickness as I was taken into hospital on Mothering Sunday due to the sickness being so bad.

Mum took some pictures of my stomach with her as my stomach keeps swelling up like balloon and going very hard.

The doctor wants me to have a gastric emptying study done; this procedure will be done by the nuclear medicine physician using radioactive chemicals that will measure the speed with which my food empties from my stomach and enters the small intestines.

When I have the gastric study done I will have to eat a meal, normally scramble egg on toast is given, which will be mixed with a small amount of radioactive material. I will also be given some fluid to drink, which will also have a small amount of radioactive material. A scanner will be placed over my stomach to monitor the amount of radioactivity in my stomach for several hours after I have eaten the meal. As the food empties my stomach, the amount of radioactivity in the stomach should decrease. The rate at which the radioactivity leaves my stomach will reflect on the rate the food is emptying from my stomach.

I have got to continue with all my medication, including the antibiotic erythromycin and the Domperidone. The doctor also wanted some blood test doing and as everyone who has followed my story knows, needles and me just don't go together. Mum came in with me while I had my blood test and I asked the nurse to close the door in case I frightened anybody waiting outside by my screams. I stuffed my jumper in my mouth to muffle the scream. But I only gave a little scream as the nurse who did the blood test managed to find a vain to get the blood on her first attempt. Mum said I did really well.

When I got home from the hospital I went to the doctor's with my mum as she keeps getting a lot of kidney infection, which just won't clear up. While I was with my mum at the doctors, mum asked my doctor if she would look at my arm as I have had a painful lump in my arm that is made worse by my crutches rubbing on it. Four weeks ago the lump was only the size of a pea and now it's the size of a conker. My doctor said it would be best if I have the lump removed so she is sending me to see a plastic surgeon.

The pain in my back has been really bad recently and I have had to result to wearing my back brace more. Mum said she would contact my spinal doctor to find out what is happening.

8th May 2010:
The pain in my back has been really bad and my back brace is too small for me now. Mum phoned the hospital to book an appointment for a new casting, but I can't go until the 9th June, I will just have to slim down. The trouble is, even after I have been for the casting for my back brace I still have to wait about four weeks for it to come back, and even then it takes a couple of visits before I get the brace. The good news is I will have it before I go away.

13th May 2010:
I spent most the morning at hospital today having my

pre' op' check in preparation for the operation on my knees. It looks like my operation will take place late June or early July as I am going away in September for two weeks and the nurse who did my pre' op' check said I will not be able to fly for up to six weeks after my operation – this could be even longer with me having both my knees done at the same time. She is going to phone me when she has spoken to the doctor who is doing the surgery. I was expecting to have a blood test so my mum put some Emla cream (magic cream) on my arm, but when I went in to see the nurse she never mentioned the blood test and I was not going to remind her. She had been told that I don't like needles and said that they will make sure they have some of the magic cream to put on my arm on the day I come into hospital for my operation. My blood pressure and everything else was ok, just have to keep my fingers crossed now that I am not still carrying the MRSA bug. I was very unwell on the way to the hospital and kept being sick, I'll be glad when I have had this gastric study done and maybe they can put me on the correct medication, which will help with this sickness.

When I got home a letter had come for me from Buckingham Palace. When I opened it, inside was an invite to The Queen's garden party on the 22nd June for both my mum and me. So I have got something nice to look forward to. The letter states that we must wear a dress and a hat and unfortunately we cannot take any pictures, as they will not let you take your camera in to the grounds of the palace.

28th May 2010:
I received a phone call from the hospital last week to say that my operation will have to be put back yet again as I am still carrying the MRSA bug, I am back on

treatment for three weeks. They cannot do the operation while I am carrying the MRSA bug as if this infection got into my blood stream it could be very dangerous.

The tumour on my arm has grown again and I have received an appointment to see the surgeon on the 17th June (the day after my grandma's birthday).

2nd June 2010:
I went for my first swab this morning to see if I am still carrying the MRSA bug, I won't get the results for a few days, Mary, my nurse, asked me to come back next Monday for my next one as I have got to have three clear swabs before I can have the operation on my knees.

I have just had a load of wristbands made for my charity so when you get time take a look on my web page and see if you would like to buy one, every penny from the sale of my wristbands goes to "When You Wish Upon a Star".

5th June 2010:
I have now finished university for the summer, and I sat my last exam today. I was not over keen on this exam if I am being honest. I will get my grades in July sometime.
I am now deciding what to do over the summer to keep me busy, with charity and hobbies.

I know I am due an operation over the summer, but I keep failing my pre-op, but hopefully I will pass it soon and I can have the operation before I go on holiday with my mum and dad.

13th June 2010:
I went for the casting for my new back brace last Wednesday, as my other one was too small. You should have seen the outfit that Paul and Keith (the guys doing

the casting for my brace) made for me, they put two white stockings over my body and one on my head to keep my hair out of the way – I looked like a Mummy from a horror film. My mum took some pictures on her phone. They then wrapped me in plaster cast to get the correct mould for my brace. I have decided to go for a white brace this time much to the disappointment of Keith and Paul; they wanted me to have one with teddies on it, which they nearly talked me into.

Unfortunately my new brace will not be ready in time for me to travel to The Queen's garden party, so I will have to hope they let me into Buckingham Palace with all my pain-killing tablets.

23rd June 2010:
Last week I went to see the plastic surgeon about the tumour in my arm, the doctor looked at my arm and agreed it should be removed as the tumour is growing, he also looked at some of the tumours that are just under the skin in my tummy and back, which are giving me some pain due to the band on my trousers pressing on them. He is also going to remove them at the same time. He was going to do the operation under a local anaesthetic but because I have a phobia of needles he is going to do the operation under a general anaesthetic. The operation should be done before I go away in September. I have now had two clear swabs from my MRSA bug and I had my 3rd swab taken last Monday, I just need that one to be clear too and then the doctor can make arrangements to do the operation on my knee.

I have got the date for my gastro test, my first one is on Wednesday 21st July, I have got to attend the Neurogastroenterology unit. I am having a hydrogen breath test, which is to investigate whether there is a bacterial overgrowth in the small intestines. I have got to drink a glucose solution and then give three samples at ten-minute intervals, by blowing into a tube. The test will take about three and half hours to do. I just hope I can keep the solution down, as the sickness is really bad at the moment.

My second test is on the 27th July in the same unit and is called a lactose intolerance test. This involves me drinking a glass of sweet liquid (lactose) after which I have got to blow into a tube every 30 minutes to collect samples of my breath. This test will take 4 hours 30 minutes. I have then got to make an appointment with Dr Watts to get the results.

24th June 2010:
I went to see Dr I Lieberman this morning at the pain clinic, I had to wear my old back brace as my back is really giving me some pain at the moment. Dr Lieberman is arranging for me to have another spinal scan using the contrast dye and I go back and see him in six months. I should get my new back brace on the 7th July, which should help with the pain in my back.

10th July 2010:
I went for my new back brace but it needed some more work doing on it, I have got to go back on the 28th July when it will be finished. Keith did want me back sooner but I have got so many hospital visits over this next three weeks it's really difficult for me to fit in.

The sickness has been really bad too so the sooner I have these other tests the better, then maybe I can start on some treatment that will help with the sickness.

1st August 2010:
The last few weeks have been pretty busy with one thing or another. I have been back and to the hospital having test or attending appointments.

I have now got my new back brace, which is much

better than my last one, Keith and Paul did a good job this time (the guys who measured me for the back brace).

I have had both my breath tests: one was to see if I was lactose intolerance and the other was to see if I had a bacterial overgrowth, can't say I enjoyed the stuff that I had to drink for either test. I was a little sick after the first test but was able to carry on with the test and I am pleased to say both tests came back clear. The sickness is no better and I still continue to be sick almost every day. I am due back to see Dr Watts at the end of August when I will find out what happens next.

I received a letter off Dr Sue Huson who has now received the results of my dyslexic test. Dr Sue Huson wants to see both my mum and me at the end of August to chat about how our health is doing.

My mum phoned the hospital last week to try and find out what was happening about the operation on my knees as I have now had three clear results from the MRSA bug that I had and the operation on my knees can now go ahead. Unfortunately, the doctor has now said that I cannot have the operation on my knees before I go away as I will not be able to fly for six weeks after surgery. Mum told him that she was told it was only two weeks but the doctor said because I was having both knees done that it would be six weeks before he would allow me to fly due to the risk of me getting a blood clot. He is now looking at doing the surgery in September, which is a bit of pain as I start back at university then, we will just have to see how things go I suppose.

It does not look as though the operation on my arm and tummy will take place until after I get back from holiday either for the same reasons, but I will know more about that operation next week after my mum has spoken with the doctor who is doing the operation.

I went for the scan on my spine last week as the pain is getting worse. I was told that I would be having a needle, which I was not happy about; mum got a tube of magic cream for me so that the needle would not hurt. When I went in for the scan and I mentioned how scared I was of injection the doctor doing the scan decided he would not use the dye, which meant I got away with having the injection.

29th August 2010:
I went to see Dr Watts last week. Dr Watts is the doctor who I see for my gastroparesis, I have not seen Dr Watts since I was in hospital as I normally see one of her registrars, anyway. Dr Watts was really nice and we had a chat about how things had been going over the past few months and she gave me the results of both my last breath tests, which have come back clear. So I am not allergic to milk and I don't have an infection in my stomach.

After telling Dr Watts how my sickness had been she said that it was important that I came into hospital when the sickness gets really bad, I told her that I felt silly coming into a busy A&E department just with sickness when there are people who are bleeding to death sitting in the waiting room.

Dr Watts said that it was very important that I came to hospital as if I got too dehydrated it could be very dangerous for me with my condition, and that if it made me feel any better she would write a letter for me saying that I suffer from a severe form of gastroparesis and that she (Dr Watts) has asked me to come into A&E department when the sickness gets bad and that she must be informed that I am in the hospital. Dr Watts is going to send me the letter to keep. I have got to go back and see Dr Watts in three months.

I also saw Dr Sue Huson this week, if you

remember Dr Sue Huson is my NF doctor and as I had not seen her for a while she said that she needed to see both my mum and me. We were running late like normal due to my transport being late, which was not the driver's fault; I am really grateful to the ambulance drivers who take me to all my hospital appointments.

Dr Sue Huson gave both my mum and me a good medical; mum had a couple of tumours that were giving her some pain and she's going to see if they can be removed. Mum also baffled Dr Sue Huson as to why her lips were so blue; Dr Sue Huson admitted that it was a new one on her. So if anyone else with NF gets blue lips please let me know.

My medical went OK, the weakness in my feet were no better and Dr Sue Huson said that it was important that I was kept an eye on every six months due to my NF being so complex and how it has affected things.

I had no new problems with my NF so I don't have to go back for another six months now.

21st September 2010:
I am now home after having two weeks away in Florida with my parents. Unfortunately, I still had a few bouts of being sick and I had to make sure that I carried a paper bag around with me. I still had a nice time while I was away.

Unfortunately, I took poorly on the flight home, the stewards asked over the speaker if anyone with medical knowledge was on the flight, a nurse came forward and I was put on oxygen for the rest of the flight home and given aspirin to thin my blood. The pilot asked to be kept informed as he was going to divert to the nearest airport so that I could be taken off the flight and taken to hospital, but I was OK. They arranged for the flight to be met by a paramedic who came on board the flight and carried out my observations. He then rang for an ambulance to meet the flight and take me to hospital; my mum came with me in the ambulance. I spent the rest of the day in hospital with my mum and dad by my side. They think that I might have had a blood clot but they were not sure. The doctor said having the aspirin will have thinned my blood and may have dissolved the clot.

I am busy getting ready for going back to university and working on my next charity event at the moment.

I have now received the letter from Dr Watts to take with me to hospital when my sickness gets really bad; I just hope I never need to use it.

11th October 2010:

I have now have the dates for the two operations that I need: the first one will be done on the 23rd October, which is a Friday, this operation will involve me having five to six tumours removed; the second operation will take place on the 22nd November when I will have an operation on both my knees. The operation will be done by keyhole surgery and I have been told it will take eight to twelve weeks to recover from the surgery.

I have got to go for my pre-operative assessment on the 22nd October to make sure I am not still carrying the MRSA bug, if I am, the operation will not be able to go ahead.

No real change with the sickness, I have my good days and bad days when I am not able to keep anything down.

On the 16th October I am at the Children's Hospital for a full body scan, my mum is going to come with me for this scan, I just hope I don't have to have any needles.

Between my operations I have arranged a charity spookathon on the 6th November where I will be staying in a haunted place overnight. Many of my ambulance drivers and other people involved in my medical care will doing the event with me, along with Danny Morris who was one of the X Factor finalist when he was part of the boy band Eton Road; Danny is now a solo artist and continues to support me at my events.

17th October 2010:
I am at hospital on Thursday for my pre-op check, which is to make sure I am OK to have my operation on Friday. On this first operation the doctor will try and remove five tumours that are giving me some pain and on Friday I have to go for another pre-op, which is to make sure I am OK for my knee operation on the 22nd November. All being well I should only be in hospital overnight for this first operation.

I had my full body-scan, my mum came with me. The scan took just over an hour and this time it really hurt my back to keep still for so long. I have got to wait to see Dr Sue Huson for the results.

5th November 2010:
I have not got the results back from my scan yet I am still waiting to hear back from Dr Sue Huson; I have asked my mum to email her for me. The operation I had to remove the tumours went OK. My mum came down to support me through this, as she knows I am quite scared, mainly of the needles if I am honest. When I was on the ward the nurse did the basic checks. After a few hours I was taken down to the theatre for the operation. My mummy came down with me and was there throughout everything and held my hand when I had my needles; when they tried to give me the needle the first time it popped my vain, and it really hurt. They eventually found a vain and managed to get the canola in. Mum was sent out of the room, and I don't

remember much more until I woke up in recovery.

I was in a bit of pain after the operation. The doctor injected some more local anesthetic into my wounds to help take the pain away. The doctor said that the tumour in my leg had grown into the muscles of the leg and was more difficult to remove; the tumour in my arm had also grown into the muscle and again was more difficult to remove. I was left very badly bruised after this surgery.

I received a call this week from the Manchester Royal Infirmary to say that the surgery on my knees has been put back yet again due to me still having a positive MRSA test when I went for my pre-op check. My mum rang the hospital to say that I recently had three swabs done at my GP surgery and one at my local hospital the day before and they had all come back negative, the hospital are now looking at the test results again. My mum has got to ring the hospital again next week after the surgeon has looked at the results.

I have been really poorly with the sickness this past week as I have not been able to keep any fluid down.

12th November 2010:
I have still not got a date for my knee operation and until this puzzle about the MRSA bug I will not have the operation done.

I had to go to A&E yesterday as the sickness had got really bad again and I had not been able to keep anything down for days. I was given an ant-sickness injection, a bag of IV fluid, and allowed to go home later in the day. I have been a little better today but I have not had much fluid, as I don't want to start being sick again.

3rd November 2010:
A few weeks on from my recent surgery, the areas that

had been operated on were still hurting, I had the stitches hanging out and I kept catching them on my clothes.

I have been in so much pain with my back and I have a few important questions that I want to ask Mr Neil Oxborrow. I have not seen Mr Neil Oxborrow for ages; he had an accident with his wrist and needed an operation so was off work for a long time, but it's nice to know he is back in work and doing well. I have got the weekend to try and find something for his dog, I always get something for his dog when I go and see him.

The last results that I had for my MRSA showed that I still have the MRSA bug and that it's the swab that they do up my nose that keeps coming back positive. I am now waiting to find out if the surgery on my knees can still be done while I have the MRSA bug.

I have been in so much pain with the tumour to the back of my knee that I have been reduced to tears, which is not like me.

21st December 2010:

My appointment with my spinal doctor (Mr Neil Oxborrow) went well yesterday. While I was waiting to see him I decided to write a message on his white board, I just wrote:

To Mr Neil Oxborrow wishing you a very Merry Christmas and a Happy New Year from your number one.

Everyone that came in read it and started laughing, I'm pleased my message cheered people up. I told Mr Neil Oxborrow I had written a message on his whiteboard and he went out to read it and even he came back with a smile on his face.

Anyway back to my appointment... Mr Neil Oxborrow showed me the x-rays that were taken last year, which showed no progression of the small degree of proximal junctional kyphosis. Mr Neil Oxborrow said I was reviewed at their x-ray meeting and it was felt that surgery was probably not the way ahead at the moment.

Mr Neil Oxborrow and I agreed to simply observe my spine for the time being. The plan now is to see Mr Neil Oxborrow in nine months with a further x-ray on arrival, and if things have got any worse at this time I may have to re-think about having the surgery. But this would be a very big operation with no guarantee of it helping with the pain. If I get to the point that I can't cope with the pain he will look at things again.

I wanted to know when I decide to have children will I be able to have a normal pregnancy and delivery or will the titanium rods make a difference to how things go. Mr Neil Oxborrow said that I would be able to have a normal pregnancy, but I may find my back is more painful, which is not uncommon for any woman having children, he did not think that I should have any problems carrying a baby to full term. He did say that he was unsure about me having an epidural due to the tumours on the spine. He did not think the pain-killing tablets that I am on would be safe to take during pregnancy. If, when I am ready to start a family and my back does worsen, I can always elect to have my delivery by caesarean section to prevent more strain on my back.

After our chat we wished each other a Merry Christmas and I asked him for a photo, which he said of course I could take his picture as long as I did not make him look fat.

Mr Neil Oxborrow mentioned that he was trying to set up a charity for scoliosis awareness and asked if I was going to send a copy of my book to help people with scoliosis. I told him I would do anything I could to help him. I gave him a bone to take home for his dog, I just cannot go and see Mr Neil Oxborrow without taking something for his dog, we go back a long way.

I was waiting for the ambulance to pick me up after my appointment (not my normal guys), an hour passed then another and another, and I was getting very stressed out and just wanted to get home. I said to my mum in a very stroppy voice, "right, that's it I have had enough of waiting". Mum said, "Sit down and stop being so bloody moody". "I'll give it another 10 minutes," I said. "Well, you don't have to" Mum said "they are here", "about time I mumbled". We finally left the hospital at 7pm and finally arrived home at 8.30pm. I was in a lot of pain as I did not have any of my medication with me and I was really tired not to mention being hungry, as I had not eaten all day.

2011

6th January 2011:
I went to see Dr Lieberman (pain specialist) today, we had a general chat and Dr Lieberman asked me how my fundraising was going? I told him about the charity band night I am having in Wrexham at the end of April and about the bands that I have coming along to perform on the night. Dr Lieberman told me about a young guy called Thom who he knows and put me in contact with him. Thom sings mainly soul and blues music. I am now chatting with him about events that I have planned.

In regards to my treatment, he is not going to mess about changing any of my medication as I am coping reasonably well on what I am taking. The only other thing that was mentioned was the subject of me having children and taking gabapentin in the future. Dr Lieberman said I would have to stop taking the gabapentin, but if the pain got really bad that I could take morphine. The safety of taking gabapentin during pregnancy has not been established but my doctor does not recommend me to take it during pregnancy. When the time comes for me to start thinking about having a family he will talk more about how the morphine will work for me.

17th January 2011:
I am still attending hospital weekly for my hypnotherapy, which is meant to help control my sickness (Gastroparesis). Gastroparesis is a condition that occurs when the stomach takes too long to empty what you have eaten.

Normally the stomach contracts to move your food down into the small intestines for it to digest. In a person suffering from Gastroparesis the vagus nerve, which controls the movement of food from the stomach into the digestive tract, has been damaged causing the muscles of the stomach and the intestines not to function properly. Due to this I am still having many days when I am constantly being sick when I have any fluids. The hypnotherapy is not helping me at the moment. I still have about eight more weeks to do, so I suppose it is early days yet.

I had to have some ketamine for the pain in my back the other night, my mum came into my room and asked me what was wrong; my mum always knows when my pain is really bad and I asked her if she would get me some ketamine as the pain was so bad.

26th January 2011:
I went to see my gastro doctor this morning (Dr Watts), Dr Watts is being really nice now and we chatted for a while, I explained that things were not much better and that I had not noticed any benefit from my weekly

hypnotherapy sessions. But as I said to Dr Watts I will give anything a try and I still have six weeks to go with my hypnotherapy. Dr Watts explained that mine was a complicated case due to my NF, which is why I am seeing her and not any of her Reg' doctors. When I first met Dr Watts over two years ago now, I was not keen on her. When I was in the hospital back in April 2009 (I was in hospital for over four weeks) Dr Watts came into my room and shouted at me for doing my college work, which still needed to be done whether I was in hospital or not. But now Dr Watts is really nice and she's mellowed so much since our first meeting.

Imagine having a stomach flu that never goes away, endless bouts of nausea and vomiting up undigested food, bloating of the stomach and food washing up into your mouth. That is what gastroparisis is like for me. One minute my tummy is flat the next I look as so I am nine months' pregnant.

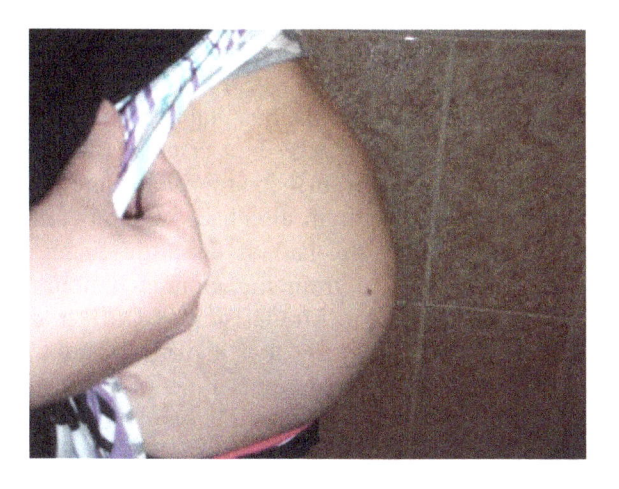

Gastroparesis, also called delayed gastric emptying, is a medical condition consisting of a paresis (partial paralysis) of the stomach, resulting in food remaining in the stomach for a longer period of time than normal. Normally, the stomach contracts to move food down into the small intestine for digestion. The vagus nerve controls these contractions. Gastroparesis may occur when the vagus nerve is damaged and the muscles of the stomach and intestines do not work normally. Food then moves slowly or stops moving through the digestive tract.

Dr Watts wants me to try Colofac, one tablet three times a day for the next six weeks to see if it helps with the bloating. Colofac is normally used for IBS (irritable bowel syndrome); I also had to have a blood test "I'm terrified of injections. They hurt like hell! The syringe reminds me of a medieval torture instrument, and the needles are far too long!" My mum came in the room with me and I think I must of almost broke her fingers as I squeezed her hand that hard, "Sorry Mum". Dr Watts said she would write to me if there was anything wrong with the blood results.

27th January 2011:

I was on the other side of the hospital bed this evening, I was visiting my mum who had just had surgery to remove five tumours from her arms that were giving her a lot of pain. My mum also had a glomus tumour removed from under the nail of her little finger; the pain my mum was in from the glomus tumour was excruciating. The doctor (Mr Christopher Duff) told my mum that it's only recently that it came to light that glomus tumour are very common in people who suffer from NF. Glomus tumours are small, benign but painful tumours. My mum had had numerous visits to different health care providers in the past, with various diagnoses documented in her medical records. Mr Christopher Duff took one look at my mum's finger and diagnosed a glomus tumour, surgery was done. This confirmed the diagnosis and resolved my mum's symptoms.

One of my mum's arms is really black and swollen from the surgery. My mum was in hospital overnight and was told she must go back if the swelling to her arm gets any worse. The doctor also told my mum that he would have a chat with her when she comes back to clinic and show her the scans that she had done, she may need to have more surgery on her right hand due to a number of painful tumours in the right hand.

7th February 2011:
The sickness has been really bad these past few weeks, and I had an allergic reaction to some antibiotics that I was put on for a water infection that I have at the moment, I had to go to A&E and they changed the antibiotic.

I go for a fitting for my new back brace and knee braces soon so maybe things will be better then.

The doctor, who is doing the operation on my knees, wants to explain what the implications will be if I have the operation while I have the MRSA bug and the risk involved in doing surgery while I have this bug.

15th February 2011:
Last week I saw the neurosurgeon doctor (John) at St Mary's, after giving me a full check over he looked at my legs that I had mentioned had been really painful. I have a large tumour in the leg that is growing. The doctor wants to make sure that this tumour can be removed safely and that it is not going to cause any nerve damage.

Just as Dr Sue Huson (my NF doctor) was about to come in the room the fire alarms went off, so we had to wait a further 20 minutes before we could continue with my appointment. The noise from the alarm was really loud and you could not hear yourselves talk.

I am being referred to see Mr Christopher Duff: a plastic surgeon, and in fact he is the doctor who recently carried out the surgery on my mum.

My mum went to the dressing clinic to have her stitches out after the operation she had to remove five tumours, but unfortunately the operation she had on her right arm had not healed and she had to go back the following week to have the stitches out, which again, had still not healed and although the nurse took the running stitch out they had to put strip stitches across her arm, which is still a little swollen and bruised.

I have not been so well with the sickness again recently, I am not able to keep anything down and I am beginning to feel warn out again with it at the moment.

21st February 2011:
I am really pleased to have my book out and for others to be reading my journey with Neurofibromatosis and Scoliosis. It does feel a little weird though to see my book in print. I have received a lot of good feedback from people who have read my book, some from people who can relate closely to what I have experienced with NF and others who just want to learn more about NF.

The book is just the beginning for me, I have got so much more planed, getting there may be a rough road at times but I'm not going to let NF stop me, and together we can help each other.

The sickness got really bad and I ended up in hospital with dehydration, I was only in overnight. I was given five bags of IV Fluid and more anti-sickness injections.

28th February 2011:
This morning I was asked to do a radio interview about

my book at BBC Radio Manchester, with Heather Scott. I also went to the M.R.I regarding having the operation on my knees.

I was at the hospital most of the afternoon and my ambulance driver (Jill) called back for me three times before I was ready to go home.

The doctor I saw had not seen me before and knew nothing about my condition (I do wish you kept to the same doctor each time). This appointment was meant to be so the doctor could talk about the risk of having surgery while I have the MRSA bug. But this doctor said he knew nothing about the MRSA and decided to look at my knees, which he said were out of line (which I already knew), he decided to send me to have x-rays on the knees, another 30 minutes later and back in to see the doctor who put the x-rays of my knees up onto the computer for me to see. He said that one knee was sitting OK but the other was well out of line. My consultant came into the room and asked what was happening, he looked at my x-rays and said to the doctor that was dealing with me "I hope you have ordered a MRI scan for this lady" and that is how it was left. I have now got to have another MRI scan of both knees before any decision is made on how to do the surgery. The doctor also thinks I may have arthritis in my knees.

Later in the week I had to go and see Paul (the guy who makes my back brace) over having a new back brace made along with two new knee braces. This appointment went really well and we sat and chattered to Paul for a while just filling him in with what's been happening.

I have also received a letter saying I have got to go for a full spinal scan in April.

The sickness is not much better really and the

hypnotherapy has not done anything to help with the sickness, but I gave it a try.

22nd March 2011
I had to go and see Mr Christopher Duff (plastic surgeon), we had a chat about some of the new tumours that I have and it was decided that they should be removed; he was going to do the operation at the end of April but I have got a charity event and I don't want to let anyone down so I said I will have the surgery after my event.

23rd March 2011:
I went to see Dr Watts who is my gastro' doctor, not much to say about this appointment really as there was no change in my condition, I am still being sick and the hypnotherapy that I was having did not help so it's been decided that I won't go anymore. I have got to go back and see Dr Watts in six weeks, or before if things get too bad with the sickness.

I have been back in hospital this month (overnight) with the sickness; I was given anti-sickness injections and IV fluids.

31st March 2011:
I had to go and see Dr Phil Bullen, at St Mary's Hospital to have a chat about the effect that the NF might have on me when I decided to have children; this appointment left me with a lot to think about.

The hospital would monitor me closely. I won't be allowed any medication and have been told I will have to stop taking my gabapentin and ketamine three months before I start trying for a baby. It may be possible to put me on morphine patches if the pain gets really bad.

I might not be able to have natural birth and would be looking at me having a cesarean section. I can't have the epidural due to the amount of tumours on my spine.

I have to accept the baby would probably be born two to three months early due to the pressure of carrying a baby would have on my health. They said once the baby is delivered they can take over and do the things for the baby that my body would not be able to do.

I really love children and one day I would love to have my own children. I also hope to open my home to foster children and adopt some children too. But for now I'll continue to take one day at a time and just enjoy life.

April 2011:
I had a great 21st Birthday, which I spent in Tenerife. I would like to say a big thank you to all my friends and family for all the lovely cards and gifts that I received, I loved each and every one of them.

It's been a busy month with the hospital again. The day I returned home from my holiday (Friday) I had to go to hospital for scans on my knees and a full spinal scan. While I was on holiday I was in so much pain with my back that I texted my mum and asked her to ring my spinal doctor to ask if I could see him before September. He is seeing me next Monday and hopefully he will have the results of my scan too.

I have been back to have my spinal brace made and I am just waiting on it coming back now, I have gone for a red one this time with black inside. When I arrived back home from the fitting of my back brace I was in so much pain and felt so unwell that I tried to get into see my GP but unfortunately the surgery was closed so my mum took me to the walk-in centre; they said they could not see any more people. They asked me what was wrong and told me to go to the A&E department. On arrival, my temp was 37.9 and the nurse said I would not have to wait very long as she could see I was in a lot of pain: two hours later the doctor called me in, I could barely walk I was in so much pain in my leg/foot and tummy.

The doctor asked for a quick rundown on my medical history and as soon as he found out I had NF he said the pain was down to my NF. I got very upset as he had not even looked at my leg or tummy and I asked why it was when he knew that I had NF did he not bother to look at my leg and just presumed that the pain must have something to do with my NF. By this time I was very upset by it all and I was in so much pain. He just said he was not going to x-ray my leg or do anything with it, but wanted to take some blood tests to try and find out why my temp was so high. The nurse came back and told me that I was being moved to a ward while I waited for my results, I have a big phobia of needles and told her I did not want any blood test doing. Mum spoke with the doctor and explained about the difficulty that I have with needles and said she would take me home and take me to see my GP in the morning. The doctor then decided to do an x-ray before allowing me home, which did not show any brakes, but I could have told him that.

The next day I went to see my GP who did examine my leg and said she was writing to Dr Sue Huson to have a look at my leg, and to my spinal doctor to try and find out what is going on. Over the weekend the pain did ease a little.

My first book is continuing to sell well and can now be bought in WH Smiths in the Trafford Centre, Manchester.

4th May 2011:
I went to Salford Royal Hospital this afternoon to have another fitting for my back brace. When Paul tried the brace on me he could not get over how well it fitted, I have not got the brace yet as it still needs the straps putting on it but I should have it in two weeks. Paul asked about my book and how it was doing, I had a copy of my book with me and Paul asked if he could buy it to put in the department. So if you are ever at Salford Royal you may just see my book.

9th May 2011:
I was at Salford Royal Hospital this afternoon to see my favourite doctor, Mr Neil Oxborrow. I had been getting a lot of pain in my back so Mr Neil Oxborrow saw me earlier than he should have done. I was sent for an x-ray of my spine, Mr Neil Oxborrow said that he would have to discuss my x-ray results at his x-ray meeting and if things look to have got worse with my spine since my last x-ray he will bring me back in to have a chat about what to do next, otherwise he will arrange for me to have extensive physio and arrange to see me in three months to see if the physio helped.

We had a chat about what I was doing at college and I could not leave without giving him a bone for his dog; he now blames me for getting his dog fat, "Sorry Neil, but it's not me who got your dog fat". I think you should take it for a run before you start work every morning, lol.

12th May 2011:
Went into hospital this morning for surgery to have five tumours removed, the operation went well and I was allowed home later in evening. I have a nice black eye from where the one on my eyebrow was removed. If anyone asks me what I have done, I tell them I had a

fight with a lamppost, its better then saying I had a tumour removed and going into all the questions that always follow. I also had tumours removed from my right thigh, abdomen, left elbow, lower back and my left eyebrow. I have the stitches removed in ten days.

Monday I am at Hope Hospital for the results of the scan I had on my knees to see if any of the tumours have grown and to chat about the surgery on my knees.

16th May 2011:

I was expecting to see Mr Khan, but saw his registrar, who did not say very much and did not look at my knees this time. The doctor put the results of my scan up on screen and I was able to take a picture of some of the report, which read as follows (I think this was the report for my left knee I can't be sure as I did not manage to get it all):

A little oedema signal in the upper parts of Hoffas fat pad, between the top of the patella tendon and the lateral femoral condyle, suggesting entrapment. The rest of the soft tissues show multiple small neurofibromata along the nerve indicating spinal phenotype NF1.

MRI Knee Rt: Standard technique. The menisci, the cruciates and collateral ligaments are intact. The patella is slightly high lying with the tendons to the patella ratio of 1.45 indicating mild patella alta. The patella lies centrally over the trochlear with a tibial tuberosity to trochlear offset of 10mm. No loose body seen. There is again a little soft tissue oedema in the top of Hoffas fat pad, close to the patella tendon and lateral femoral condyle. Multiple neurofibromata are again noted.

The report is as clear as mud to me really, but the doctor said that I needed to have some physio before any surgery is done to build up my quads. I asked if I could have the physio at my local hospital, he said it would have to be done at Hope Hospital for the first one and then they may be able to transfer me over. He then asked where I lived and said why do I come all the way up here to see Mr Khan? After going into why I had been sent to see Mr Khan he asked if I would like my treatment to be transferred over to my local hospital, to which I said, "Yes". It would make things so much easier going to my local hospital. He said he would speak with Mr Khan and ask him if it would be OK to transfer me and that he would also have to write to my local hospital and see if the doctor there would be willing to take my case on. He said my case was a complex one due to the tumours involved but he was sure between my plastic surgeon and the orthopedic doctor they could work something out.

19th August 2011:
I have been to see Dr Sue Huson at St Mary's Hospital. Not much to report really apart from having a new lump in the back of my leg that is now the size of a golf ball and feels hard. I mentioned it to Dr Sue Huson and after she had looked at it she felt it would be a good idea if I had a PET Scan to make sure it was not a nasty lump and the fact that I had not had a PET Scan for over two years she did not want to waste time by me having an MRI Scan. I should have the scan in next two weeks. The lump only really hurts if I am sitting down pressing on the lump.

What is a PET Scan?
A PET Scan, or Positron Emission Tomography Scan, is an imaging technique that allows physicians to examine many organs of the body and is helpful in diagnosing many diseases, such as cancer. Other scans such as a CT scan or MRI scans; only show organ

structure, where a PET Scanner shows organ structure and function.

The orthopedic doctor (Mr Kumar) at my local hospital has agreed to see me over the problem with my knees. I see him next week. I have so many problems with them giving way on me these past few weeks and Dr Sue Huson committed on how loose both my kneecaps were. I have been doing physio at the gym to try help but it's not helping at the moment.

23rd August 2011:
I have got the date for my PET Scan at The Christie Hospital, I go on the 31st August (my mum and dad's wedding anniversary). I have been told that I can't eat for six hours before the scan but to drink lots of water. My mum phoned the hospital this morning to confirm that I will be attending and to explain that I have a big problem with needles, they are going to use some of the magic cream before giving me the injection. I will have to decide which CD to take with me as I have got sit in a room on my own for an hour after the injection.

I have been bad with the sickness again this week and was up till after 2am this morning being sick, I thought it was settling down, but no such luck.

I have been wearing my old back brace to swim in as I was in so much pain while swimming. Wearing the brace has helped with the pain.

29th August 2011:
My appointment with Mr Kumar the orthopedic surgeon that I am now seeing went really well. I didn't see Mr Kumar but I saw his registrar who came in the room and introduced himself to my mum and me. He gave both my legs a very good examination and had me standing up on my feet. I was then told that I have flat feet and that I need insoles putting in my shoes.

What is Flat Foot?
Flat foot is a condition where the longitudinal arch or instep of the foot collapses and comes into contact with the floor. Fallen arches can also cause flat foot. Wear and tear can weaken the tendon that is responsible for shaping the arch. Fallen arches can also be caused by injury. The treatment for flat feet needs to be evaluated by a doctor or health care worker to determine the treatment.

The doctor was not sure if my NF had anything to do with my flat feet, he is sending me for physio and as I mentioned I am having shoe inserts fitted to my shoes.

If you have foot pain and think you may have flat feet, try the following test, which help determine your arch type.

1. Foot print test when your feet are wet: look at your footprint on the floor. The front of your foot will be joined to the heel by a strip. If your foot is flat, then the strip will be the same width, as the front of the foot, creating a footprint that looks stretched. With a normal arch, the strip is about half the width of the front of the foot. If you have a high arch a thin strip will connect the front of the foot with the heel.

2. Another test you can do is: put your shoes on a flat surface and view them at your eye level from behind. See if the soles of the shoes are worn evenly. A flat foot will cause more wear on the inside of the sole of the shoe, especially in the heel area. You will notice that the shoe will easily rock from side to side. A flat foot will also cause the upper part of the shoes to lean inwards over the sole. Both shoes should wear about the same way.

I don't go back to see Mr Kumar until the New Year, which will give time for the insoles to have had some effect and also the physio. He also wants to get hold of all my x-rays and scans that I have had done of my knees so he can decide if he thinks having surgery will help with my knees giving way.

I go for my PET scan on Wednesday, but will not get the results for a few days.

3rd September 2011:

Dr Sue Huson kindly emailed my mum today to say that the PET scan that I had showed no nasty tumours, this is great news and I can now go away and enjoy my holiday next week. Dr Sue Huson said she will send me a full report next week but wanted to let me know everything was OK, "Thank you, Dr Sue Huson".

I received a letter over being measured for my insoles, but I am away and will have to rearrange the appointment for when I get back from my holiday.

I have also received a letter from the Red Cross after being nominated for the Humanitarian Citizen Award (HCA): I have got to go to London on the 8th October 2011 where I will meet all the other short-listed people.

I ended up in A&E last week as I fell badly on my knees after my knee gave way on me. After having an x-ray I'm pleased to say all was OK and my knee was just badly bruised.

12th October 2011:

Today was a busy day for hospital visits, this morning I was at Withington Hospital originally to see Dr Watts, but although I did not see her the appointment went well. I normally see Dr Watts over my sickness, but things have not been too bad with my sickness recently as I have only been sick a few times over the past week or so, which is good when I think back to when I was being sick every day.

I have got to continue taking my medication and he wants me to go back onto stomach tablets that I was taking. I was meant to have a blood test but could not buck up the courage to go for it. I have really bad veins; the kind that disappear as soon as someone tries to get blood, where the nurse tries my right arm, then my left arm, then goes back to the right arm, then starts looking at my hands. By this time both my arms are bruised and I'm in tears. I'm sure you get the picture. I have tried the magic cream but it does not always work. I will probably receive a letter asking me why I have not had the blood test in a few weeks, but Dr Watts knows about my phobia and it is written on my hospital notes so I'm sure they will understand. Well, I hope they do.

Later in the morning I was at MRI seeing Mr Christopher Duff who is my plastic surgeon. When I went in to see him there were two other doctors and Joe (my NF nurse) in the room. They all introduced themselves, which helped to relax me. Mr Christopher Duff showed me the recent scans of my knees/legs and pointed out all the white dots on my scans (there were loads) and said that all the white bits I could see were the tumours in my knees and legs. I told him that I was being bothered by the tumour at the top of my thigh as it was growing and felt like a golf ball. I also have one on my back that hurts when I try to sit back on a chair. Mr Christopher Duff said he would remove them for me. He is looking at doing the surgery in December under a general anaesthetic.

13th October 2011:
Today I saw the orthotics doctor over my flat feet (what a nice guy). He fitted me with insoles in both shoes and said that both my feet were really flat. Flat foot is also known as fallen arches. A flat foot does not have an arch when standing. The doctor thinks by putting insoles in my shoes it may help with my knee and it could even help with my back pain, so fingers crossed.

My orthotic doctor said he wants to see me again in

about four weeks and that he wants me to bring my foot braces and knee braces with me, as he is going to see if he can come up with something that will be more comfortable for me.

28th October 2011:
Today, I was at the E.N.T department to have a hearing test due to the bad ear infection that I had while I was away on holiday. The good news is, I passed my hearing test and my ears were looking much better, I don't have to have the scan now, which was good news.

Yesterday, I had to go to a meeting in Manchester and my mum met me at the Royal College of Music on Oxford Road, we were just standing by the road deciding which way to go as I was early for my appointment so we had decided to go for a drink. The next minute this young man was knocked off his bike by a woman coming out of a side road, it was very upsetting to see. Mum gave the young man first aid while I called for an ambulance and directed the traffic. Another young man joined Mum who said he was in his first year training to be a doctor so he also checked him out. He was very lucky to have only hurt his leg; he was wearing a helmet which saved any head injury. The young man was talking and told us that his name was Tom. Mum then phoned one of his friends and told him what had happened and asked if he would meet the ambulance at the Manchester Royal Infirmary. One of the ambulance drivers was more worried about my mum's lips being so blue and kept asking her if she was OK. About an hour later the police rang my mum to ask if she would give a statement as to what happened, the police said Tom had been really lucky and had got away with just a leg injury.

I have got a busy week studying and sorting out my spook night that I am having in December.

17th November 2011:
I should have the date for my surgery soon; Mr Christopher Duff said he was going to do the surgery after I have had my charity event, which is only a few weeks off. I am getting really excited now, but I am not so pleased that Hyde Town Hall is charging me £562.50 to hold the event; that is a large chunk of the money raised on the night and today I have received an email to say they have cut the number of places that can go round this time. Don't think I will use Hyde Town Hall for my next ghost hunt.

My mum had to go and see Mr Christopher Duff last week over the surgery he did on her hand, pleased to say the surgery went well. He is going to do more surgery on my mum in the New Year as she has got a few tumours at the back of her knees that give pain when she has her knee braces on. Mr Christopher Duff is one of the best plastic surgeon I have ever met; you cannot even tell that my mum had surgery on her hand and he is a really nice guy at making you feel at ease.

15th December 2011:
I have been pencilled in to have surgery on the 22nd December; I am having about five tumours removed. But at the moment my sickness is really bad and I have been in a lot of pain with my tummy. I have got to go for a pre-op check on Friday to make sure they can still do the surgery.

2012

3rd January 2012:
I have had a few busy weeks over the Christmas holidays.

I had entered a competition to be a VIP guest at The North Pole Bar, to see a young man perform, called

Lloyd Daniels. Lloyd is an amazing singer. He was in the X Factor in 2009 and got through to the final six. I was gutted when he went, so when I heard about his gig where only 50-100 people could go I had no hesitation in applying. I received a call the day before to say that I had been picked. My mum and I went along to watch Lloyd sing and we sat at the front watching him. At the end of the gig Lloyd took time to talk to all his fans one by one and in a group. I have lots of pictures taken with Lloyd. I got talking to Lloyd and we exchanged phone numbers. I was kind of shocked that Lloyd asked me for my number but I was not going to complain, or say "No".

I went into hospital on the 22nd December 2011. I was up really early to go to the hospital for my operation. I was not looking forward to the needles, as many of you know I'm scared of them. But I had some magic cream with me; I had my music and phone to keep me company whilst I was waiting to go down. My mum also stayed with me.

When I arrived at the hospital I signed in and sat down to wait to see a doctor. Whilst I sat watching *Day Break* on TV I had a call from a lovely young man. This was a call that I had been waiting for, for a few days; it was from Lloyd Daniels. Lloyd said he would help me out as much as he could with my charity work and that he would like to meet me for coffee, which I agreed to do once I recovered from my surgery. While I was chatting to Lloyd I was called in to see Mr Christopher Duff so had to cut my chat with Lloyd short.

I chatted with Mr Christopher Duff, about the tumours that needed removing, Mr Christopher Duff said he can only have me in theatre for one hour and he will remove what he can in order of priority. When they were knocking me out for the operation I was making everybody laugh as I kept talking about the North Pole and where I met Lloyd. They thought I had lost the plot and Mum had to tell them I met Lloyd at a bar called the North Pole.

Mr Christopher Duff was able to remove all the tumours, I was in hospital two nights as I had taken poorly and kept being sick. Mr Christopher Duff said that I might have to stay in hospital over Christmas if things don't settle down. But I came out late Christmas Eve. I had lots of visitors non-stop coming to see me. I had my own little side room so when my friends came I was able to cause trouble and have a laugh.

Christmas was very quiet; I was not feeling too good so I slept a lot of the day. Santa came to see me, which was great, so I must have been good. I received a Peter Andre Calendar. But the calendar is more or less being used as a poster around my bedroom. I would love to meet Peter Andre, fingers crossed my wish may come true one day.

I have got some really big news to tell you. I have been named on the New Year's honours list and I am to receive an M.B.E from the queen. I am still very much in shock by this news. I don't know what I have done to deserve such a big honour.

22nd January 2012:
I went to see Dr Lieberman two weeks ago, who is my Pain Consultant; as I am coping with my pain at the moment I don't have to see him for 12 months, but if my pain gets worse I can just ring him up and he will see me. Dr Lieberman congratulated me on my M.B.E and said he will do what he can to help me raise some funds for my charity. Dr Lieberman is really nice and as I have said before he makes you feel very relaxed when talking to him.

I have not been back to see Mr Christopher Duff

after my surgery yet; he said he would see me in three months. My mum is having some tumours removed next month by Mr Christopher Duff.

I received a lovely package over the weekend from Russell Watson. Russell had sent me signed copy of his DVD Live at The Royal Albert Hall, signed CD Russell Watson LA Voice, signed music score *Music of The Night* and signed photo. Russell said he had sent them for me to auction to raise money towards my target. My friend Harry Singleton had wrote and told Russell about me, Russell wrote back saying he was aware of my story and wanted to help. I am going to auction these items at my charity ball in October.

22nd February 2012:
I have now got my date for when I go to Buckingham Palace to receive my M.B.E. I am really looking forward to it. I still don't know who will be giving me my M.B.E yet and I have still got to get my outfit and hat, which will be fun.

I have just finished another few months of physio, which I am doing at home now for a while.

I went to see my orthopedic doctor a few weeks ago and he said I will at some point need surgery on both my knees, but I have got so much going on in my life at the moment and I am busy working on lots of charity events and ideas at the moment, I really have not got the free time to have the operation on my knees. As long as the pain does not get too bad I will stick it out for as long as I can before I have the surgery.

My mum was in hospital last week having some tumours removed. She was in hospital a little longer than expected due to her not being so well after surgery. Mr Christopher Duff did my mum's surgery. Mr Christopher Duff really is the very best in his field of plastic surgery and I know that both my mum and I would not let anyone else do our plastic surgery now.

I am due to see Mr Christopher Duff next month about the surgery he did on me just before Christmas.

18th March 2012:
I went to see Mr Christopher Duff last week (my plastic surgeon), I saw him at St Mary's Hospital, while I was waiting to see him I decided to have a play in the playpen and built a house out of Lego, one of the NF nurses saw me and came over for a chat she congratulate me on my M.B.E and thanked me for attending the NF meeting the week before. Jo one of the other NF nurses came out and called my name so Mum and I went in to see Mr Christopher Duff. When I went in the room Mr Christopher Duff smiled and bowed as did the other doctors who were in the room and Mr Christopher Duff said "Have I got to bow every time I see you now you have an M.B.E?", I laughed and told him "No".

We had a really nice chat and Mr Christopher Duff said the biopsies that were done on my recent surgery came back clear, which was great news; he also said that he was booking me in for some more surgery in September. While I was talking to Mr Christopher Duff the surgery door opened and it was Professor G Evans; he had heard I was in the building and wanted to say hello to me. He joked to Mr Christopher Duff and asked him if he had bowed to me yet; everyone was very relaxed and Professor G Evans told Mr Christopher Duff about the NF documentary that I had made and edited myself for part of my exams at University. Professor G Evans spoken to my mum and me about some treatment that they hope to start using for with people with NF2. The hope is, it will shrink the tumours; they are still working on treatment for people with NF1 but it's all very new at the moment and not everyone would be suitable for the treatment.

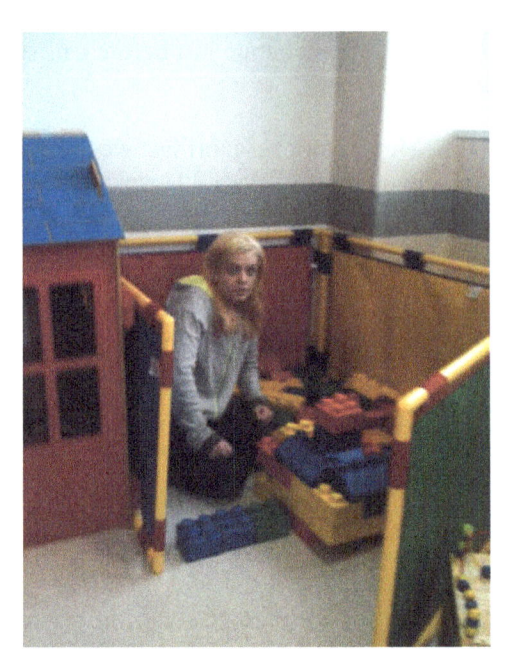

Thought you might like to see what a nutter I am.

I am still trying to get my first book on Kindle, my publisher wanted to put it on but was also going to take 50% of the royalties, which I was not going to agree to as this would take more money away from the charity.

I have got some new foot braces and knee braces; they are not as clumsy looking as the ones I was wearing. The new braces for my knees are called "Bio Skin's Q Brace" the unique design is meant to allow multidirectional traction of the patella. The "T" strap prevents dislocation and may be attached in various positions to control the direction of traction on the patella. It is made of a breathable material, which is meant to make it comfortable to wear, even in hot weather.

My drop foot splints come in two separate parts and support above the ankle and a non-slip section, which fits between the tongue and shoelaces on your footwear, the sections are linked by an adjustable elastic strap for tailored support. I can't say I am finding them easy to wear at the moment but I am going to give it a few more weeks to see how I get on with them, there are still a few more things on the market that I can try so I will just have to see how it goes.

I am off to Buckingham Palace next week to receive my M.B.E. I have not been told who will be giving me the M.B.E yet – apparently I will not be told until a few minutes before. On the Friday I have been invited to have lunch with the Lord Mayor of Manchester and have been told that The Queen and Duke of Edinburgh will be attending the event too. I am not allowed to take any pictures at any of the events but we can buy pictures taken of me receiving my M.B.E that are taken by the palace photographer.

30th April 2012:

I have been having a lot more pain in my back recently and have been wearing my back brace, I am also waiting for some new knee and foot braces, which should be in stock soon.

I am at the hospital on Wednesday to see Dr Watts about my sickness, which has not been too bad recently.

7th May 2012:

My appointment with Dr Watts went OK and I don't have to go back and see her for six months unless I start getting bad again, in which case I have got to go back sooner.

I am at the hospital tomorrow to see "Stephen" who is my Orthotic doctor; I am in hope that my new braces are ready. I am having new foot and knee braces as the other ones that I had were not doing anything to help my situation. Last time I saw Stephen I spoke about the possibility of having a different back brace made and he said he would have a word with Mr Neil Oxborrow. I have been in so much pain with my back recently and none of my tablets are helping.

16th May 2012:
I have got a busy few weeks ahead of me: I am working on my course assignment, which is about NF, I have been busy filming people, interviewing people with NF and interviewing some doctors who know about the condition Neurofibromatosis.

I have also been back to see my orthotic doctor (Stephen) over my knee, foot and back brace. The knee brace that I am trying out is called a Q Brace, this brace is to help stop my knees from dislocating and hopefully help with the pain. They are very difficult to put on and even worse to take off when knee has swollen because with this brace you have to pull the entire support (brace) passed the heel. Then, from a standing position, using both hands with a firm grip, pull and centre the support over the patella. I then have to position a "T strap" on the lateral side of the patella, all bit complicated. I am back to see Stephen next week as he has ordered some more for me to try.

I have been having a lot of pain in my back so Stephen is having a word with my spinal doctor (Mr Neil Oxborrow) to see if it would be wise to try a different kind of back brace.

4th June 2012:
I managed to get my course assignment finished, which is a short documentary about NF. I filmed people who have Neurofibromatosis, and interviewed some doctors who know about the condition Neurofibromatosis. I have got to hand my assignment in on Wednesday.

I went back to see Stephen, my orthotic doctor, to pick up my new knee and foot braces; he has still not managed to write to Mr Neil Oxborrow over my back brace yet but hopes to write this next week. The sooner the better really as I have been in a lot of pain with my back recently.

Well, it's not long off until it's my turn to do the Olympic torch. I am really looking forward to it, all I know at the moment is I am carrying the Torch in Blackpool between 5pm and 7pm on the 22nd June.

21st June 2012:
I have had a busy few days, I was having some problems with my wrist due to a new tumour growing on the wrist, my hand kept shaking and I was unsure if the new tumour had anything to do with the shaking. So when my mum went to see Mr Christopher Duff who removed some of her tumours three months back, she mentioned it to him and he said he wanted to see me the next day to make sure everything was OK.

Mum had to go to the hospital to see Stephen (our orthotic doctor) for the fitting of her new knee brace. Stephen told my mum that he had had a letter from my spinal doctor (Mr Neil Oxborrow) over my new back brace. Stephen needed to see me to discuss the letter and to measure me for the new back brace. My dad came and got me while Stephen was seeing to my mum and I was measured for a new type of back brace.

I also came down with the flu and ended up at the doctor's twice this week; the doctor wanted to start me on inhalers and steroids to help with my breathing as he said my chest was very wheezy but I mentioned that I was going away at weekend so he said that he could not start me on them as he would need to see me again the following week. I have been put on some strong antibiotics and I am beginning to feel much better.

The brace I have now is a new innovative spinal orthosis (brace) to provide support, limit motion, and decrease pain. It is intended to stabilise my back; it is still restrictive in order to prevent undesirable motion. It is hoped that this brace will help with the pain.

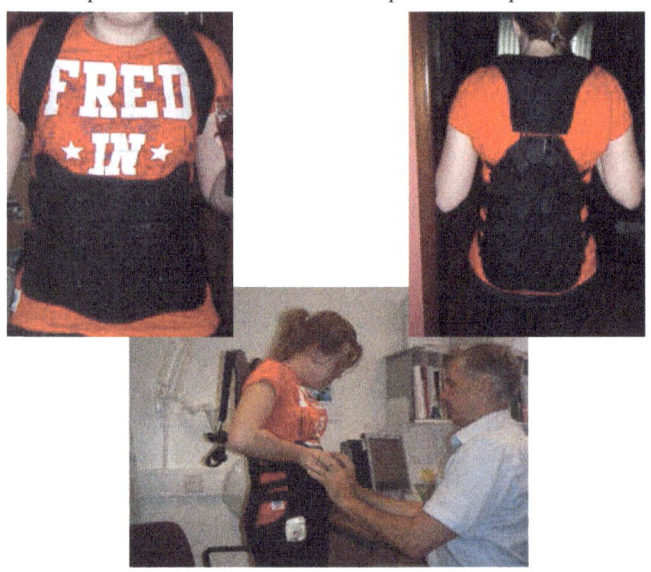

Tomorrow I have a big day ahead of me as I am carrying the Olympic torch in Blackpool along Fleetwood Road at 5.35pm; I am really excited about it, as it is such a big honour.

23rd June 2012:
Yesterday, I had an amazing day from start to finish, I carried the Olympic torch along Fleetwood Road,

Blackpool you can read more about this day later in the book.

7th October 2012:
The operation that I had on the 20th September to remove four tumours went well and Mr Christopher Duff (my plastic surgeon) managed to remove all of the tumours. I had the tumours frozen so that they could be sent away to allow research to be done on them. I had the stitches out last Sunday and apart from a little swelling from the one I had removed from my back all is looking good. Mr Christopher Duff is the best plastic surgeon I have ever had remove my tumours, he always does a great job.

I have been having a lot of pain in my knees so my appointment was brought forward to see my orthopedic doctor this week, and after having x-rays it was decided that I am to have a scan, which I will have on the 15th November. He will then decide the best way forward.

I see my orthotic doctor next week; the braces that I was given for my foot drop is not really helping so he wants to try me with a different type. I have also had some problems with my back brace, which should be sorted at the same time.

My Black and White Ball takes place next week. I have managed to get hold of some great auction prizes, which is thanks to Manchester City football Club, Manchester United Football Club, Slaters, Lorraine Kelly, Russel Watson, Peter Hook, Ken Dodd, Daniel Craig and many more.

10th November 2012:
My gastroparisis (sickness) is still bad and I'm finding it difficult to keep things down again, which is making me feel drained at the moment. I have also had a lot of pain in my back and both my knees. I am due to have a

scan of my knees next week and then the following week I am back at the hospital to see the doctor (Mr Kumar) for the results of the scan, I also see my doctor over my sickness in two weeks.

Work is going OK but I am getting very tired and my back really hurts, having to take a lot of pain medication to get through the day. I have been coming home, having tea and going to bed due to being so tired.

You can now follow me on Twitter @kirstysstory to see what I am up to and to see how my fundraising is coming along. I would love it if you would join me on Twitter.

I am also starting work at the CBBC; I have been given a six months placement, which I am really looking forward too, can't say I am looking forward to the early start. I really need a car as I can't afford to keep using taxis.

2013

11th January 2013:
Well, it's the start of a new year and a great year I had last year. Being named on the New Year's Honours' list and being awarded the M.B.E. I carried the Olympic torch in Blackpool and landed a job at Children's BBC, the only problem with the job it will come to an end in April: let's hope I can find another job within the BBC.

My brother got engaged to his long-term girlfriend (Stacey) on Christmas Day, I want to send my congratulations to them both and looking forward to being told the date of the wedding now.

I saw Mr Christopher Duff just before Christmas, he was pleased with how my last lot of surgery went that I had in September and I don't have to see him for six months now unless I have any problems in which case he will see me before.

My appointment with Mr Kumar did not go as well, he said the scan of my knees showed that the ball of my knees does not have a grove for the kneecap to sit in, but if he did surgery now it would make matters worse for me. I have got to continue wearing the knee braces to help support my knees and when my knees start popping out to the side (which they will do) he will try and do surgery or if I can't cope with the pain he will look again at what can be done to help me.

Mum and I have been asked if we will help with the year 5 OSCE Examinations on the 15th January. I have done this many times in the past and I really enjoy helping the doctors in this way and it's also helps the new doctors to understand more about NF.

I have been getting so much pain in my back, the pain medication I am currently taking have not really been helping me. I get so much pain to the top of my spine that it can bring tears to my eyes I also get a lot of discomfort lower down by my bra strap, which is more of an ache, I asked my mum if she could see any tumours in that area that my strap maybe pressing on. My mum said I do have a small tumour in that area. I did buy some sport bras to see if they would make any difference to the discomfort, but they made no change whatsoever.

12th February 2013:
I have had a busy few weeks both with work and hospital visits.

I was at the pain clinic a couple of weeks ago, Dr Lieberman was not in as he had been involved in an accident and had hurt his pelvis. I mentioned that I had been getting a lot more pain in my back and the nurse that I saw went and had chat with one of the other doctors who suggested that I contacted my spinal doctor (Mr Neil Oxborrow) as he was unsure if my back had worsened at the top, and come back to see Dr Lieberman in February when he is back in work. My mum contacted Mr Neil Oxborrow when we got home and I have got to go and see him in March. The other doctor I saw wanted me to have a scan and x-ray of my spine to be sure what is going on.

Stephen, the guy who does my spinal brace, thinks I might benefit from a new type of back brace and is going to have a chat with Mr Neil Oxborrow to see what he thinks. He did say it's a lot more expensive than the one I have now but if it helps it will be worthwhile getting me one.

Work's been really busy, but enjoyable. I went for a job interview with the charity that I raise money for "When you Wish Upon a Star" but I did not get the job, my contract is coming to an end with the BBC, I am just keeping my fingers crossed that I can find another job with the BBC.

15th March 2013:
I am seeing Mr Neil Oxborrow on Monday, as I have been in a lot of pain in my back and it seems to be getting worse. I joined a gym to do some physio and swimming in the hope it would help, but unfortunately it's not really helping. I hope Mr Neil Oxborrow can help with some advice on what to do.

My contract at the CBBC is almost at an end, I have had no luck finding another job within the BBC as yet.

19th March 2013:
I went to see my favourite doctor yesterday (Mr Neil Oxborrow), who is my spinal surgeon. It was a late appointment and traffic was really bad, as unfortunately there was a bad accident in front of us and traffic came

to a standstill. I came off the motorway early and Mum rang the hospital to explain that I might be late due to the accident. It turned out that I was only ten minutes late and when at the clinic Mr Neil Oxborrow said "Hi" to me when he saw me and said that he would see me soon and that I was last to be seen.

I went into see Mr Neil Oxborrow with my mum, and after having a chat with both my mum and me, I explained that I had been in a lot of pain at the top of my back and it had been getting worse. I also mentioned that one of my hands was cold and the other was warm, he did not think the hand being cold and other being warm was spinal related.

He brought the x-ray that I had done back in 2011 up on the computer screen, he pointed out the curve above the rods and said the pain could be due to pressure from that point. He mentioned doing more surgery by taking the rods all the way to the top; he also mentioned doing intense physio and seeing one of his spinal pain team. Mr Neil Oxborrow sent me for an x-ray and said if the spine has worsened he wants me to have a bone scan to see how the bones are at the top of the spine; he is going to phone me and let me know the results. He is not really keen to do surgery unless it is going to benefit me, which is a good thing. I have now got to wait and see if the spine has worsened from my last x-ray. The pain is so bad at times that I have to take ketamine, which I don't like as it makes me feel spaced out. I don't like being in so much pain and discomfort but I am really not sure about having more spinal surgery– not that I don't trust Mr Neil Oxborrow, I do and he is the only person I would trust to do my surgery. I will just have to see how the bone scan goes.

After my appointment I met up with Professor Gareth Evans and his wife Chris De Winters, along with Garry and Colin who have said they want to help

Children with Tumours raise lots of money.

2nd April 2013:
I have had a busy few weeks, I went away with my mum for a week and I have now heard back from my spinal doctor (Mr Neil Oxborrow).

Mr Neil Oxborrow said he had now reviewed my x-rays and that there was no real change from the last x-ray that I had, but he wants me to have a bone scan to see if there is any increased activity at the end of the metal work. He said that I have quite a long instrumentation, which is quite flat and he suspects that this is representing a stress area at the top of my spine where it turns into a mobile spine.

I am having my bone scan on the 10th April 2013, the scan will be done in the Nuclear Medicine Department and I will be having: 1. NM Bone Local Upper Limb, 2. NM Bone Local Upper Limb, 3. NM Bone SPECT and 4. NM CT Atten Correct and diagnostic study. The scan will take about four hours and I will have to have an injection, which I am not looking forward too, my mum will be with me and will be holding my hand while I have the injection.

If there is any change Mr Neil Oxborrow will bring me in for a chat, if not, I will be seeing Dr Lieberman to talk about having some aggressive rehab in the first instance. I will see Mr Neil Oxborrow when he has seen the bone scan results.

The other appointments I had waiting for me when I got home from my week away with my mum were a letter to see Dr Sue Huson (NF doctor) and Mr Christopher Duff (plastic surgeon). I am seeing Dr Sue Huson on the 23rd May and Mr Christopher Duff on the 8th May to talk about the removal of some more tumours.

I went to Spain with my mum for a week, as I had to

get away from this cold weather; we both had a lovely time and it was nice spending some quality time together.

I have been short-listed for the Inspiring Woman Award and I am in the final three in my category, I am attending an award ceremony on the 17th May.

Wish I could say the pain in my back was much better but unfortunately it's not, last night I had to get up and take my ketamine as I was in so much pain.

Not sure why one of my hands is cold and the other is warm, it's the same with my feet but they have been like that since I had my spinal surgery.

29th May 2013:

It's been pretty hectic recently, mainly with work and hospital visits.

As for the pain in my back I had my bone scan and I am now waiting for the results. I'm still in a lot of pain, I might have to have physiotherapy to help build up my muscles in my back. I'm not really sure what's going to happen, but hopefully we can find something, which helps with the pain.

Some good news: I was awarded the winner of the "Inspiring Young Woman of the Year 2013", I gave a speech and was given a standing ovation. You can read more about the event later in my book.

I saw Mr Christopher Duff about some tumours that are giving pain, we had a chat and it was decided that six tumours are best being removed; this will be done after my holidays.

I have also seen my NF doctor this week (Dr Sue Huson), we had time for a chat and a catch up as Sue had not seen me for a while and she is always interested to know what I am getting up too.

Going back to medical issues, I mentioned that I have been having problems with my memory and that I forgot my way home from work the other day. Dr Sue Huson felt it best to arrange for me to have a brain MRI scan; she is also arranging for me to have a full body scan so she can see if any of the internal tumours are growing.

Dr Sue Huson mentioned that people with NF can lack vitamin D and wanted me to have a blood test. I only had blood test yesterday at my doctor's, the nurse who was doing the blood test could not find a vain and had to ring my favourite nurse at our surgery (Mary Brennon). Mary had some problems getting blood too, but she managed to get some in the end and even gave me a smiley face on my plaster. Anyway, back to the hospital blood test... Dr Sue Huson asked me to wait in the waiting room for my name to be called, I hid in the Wendy House as I really did not want another needle, but I knew I had to have the blood test to check my Vit D. I went in the room when my name was called and the nurse doing the test said she had to ring for a porter and get an ice pack for one of the blood tests as it was down as urgent and had to be taken to the lab right away.

I was really tired when I got home and I kept being sick; my gastroparesis has flared up.

Having MRI Scan:
An MRI scan is usually carried out as an outpatient procedure. This means you will not have to stay in hospital overnight. After the scan you can resume your normal activities. However, if you needed a sedative, a friend or relative will need to take you home and stay with you for 24 hours after having the sedative. A magnetic resonance imaging (MRI) scan is a painless procedure that last 15-90 minutes, depending on the size of the area being scanned and number of images needed.

Due to the strong magnetic fields that are produced by the MRI scanner, it's very important to remove any metal objects from your body, including: watch, earrings, rings and necklace. Depending on which part of your body is being scanned, you may be asked to wear a hospital gown. If you don't want to wear a gown, remember to wear clothes without fasteners, zips and buckles.

Some scans will involve having an injection of contrast dye. The dye will make certain tissues and blood vessels show up more clearly and in greater detail. The dye is usually injected into the arm during the scan. This can make some people feel sick but this could be the thought of having an injection. Needles are scary things.

The MRI scanner is a short tunnel, which is open at both ends. You have to lie on a motorised bed that is moved inside the tunnel. You will enter the scanner either head or feet first, depending on the part of your body being scanned.

A computer is used to operate the scanner, which is located in a different room so that it is kept away from the magnetic fields that are generated by the scanner.

A radiographer operates the computer, so they will also be in a separate room from you. However, you will be able to talk to the radiographer through an intercom and they will be able to see you at all times. Normally someone can stay with you, but they will also be asked to remove metallic objects.

It's very important that you keep still during the scan to avoid the images from being blurred. At certain times during the scan, you will hear load-tapping noises. This is the electric current in the scanner coils being turned on and off. You will be given earplugs or headphones to wear. Some hospitals let you listen to a CD.

You will have to complete some paperwork ; loads of questions to answer. Most likely they will ask for a list of your medications, so just take a list of your medication with you, they also ask about previous surgeries that you have had. The reason for this is some surgeries can leave metal in your body, most surgical implants are safe but they need to be aware of them. I have two titanium rods in my spine and I have had many MRI spinal scans so don't worry about having a scan.

Your scan will need to be studied by a radiologist (a person trained in interpreting scans and x-rays) and possibly discussed with other specialist. You will not get your results from the scan immediately. The radiologist will send the report to the doctor who arranged for you to have the scan.

One tip for you: if you have a lot of back pain or headaches, take a pain reliever prior to the scan. Lying flat for 20-90 minutes can make your back sore.

Good luck, I am sure you will find that having a scan really is not that bad, close your eyes and think of something nice.

6th June 2013:

I received a letter from Mr Neil Oxborrow over the bone scan that I had, Mr Neil Oxborrow said he had now reviewed the scans and is making an outpatient appointment so he can discuss the scans further with me. My back is so painful; I have had difficulty sleeping, which is making me really tired in the day. I have been taking my strong painkilling medication, which I don't really like to take as they make me feel spaced out. I don't see Mr Neil Oxborrow till August; I just hope I can cope with the pain till then.

1st August 2013:
I received a letter from Dr Sue Huson, over the visit I had with her on the 24th May. Dr Sue Huson was pleased that other than the foot-drop there were no signs of any change to the strength or sensation in my arm or legs, which was encouraging. Dr Sue Huson still wants me to see Gemma Mercer who I have seen before due to how bad my memory is getting. I think I saw Gemma when I was tested to see if I was dyslexic. I was diagnosed with dyslexia a few years back now, don't know why it's taken so long as I always struggled at school in my English class and my English teacher at the time said he thought I was dyslexic.

What is Dyslexia?
Dyslexia is not a disease it is a condition that you are born with, so there is no cure.

Once you have been told you have dyslexia it will be present throughout your life. Dyslexia mainly affects reading and language skills and the effects can range from mild to very severe. The sooner dyslexia is spotted, the sooner strategies can be put into action.

Dyslexia can be treated. A person with this learning disorder simply needs some extra support. People who are faced with dyslexia can be successful students and successful in their adult life; they will find their own way of doing things and there are many successful famous people who are dyslexic.

I was the first person in our family to go to university, my family is really proud of me and I am happy I have achieved what I wanted to do.

The blood test that I had to check my vitamin D and bone biochemistry was normal. Vitamin D is important for good health, growth and strong bones. A lack of vitamin D is very common in people who suffer from NF.

4th August 2013:
I went for my full body scan this morning, which was far too early on a Sunday morning. I had to be at the children's hospital in Manchester for 8am. The scan took over an hour. I rang up the department a few days before, as I was worried about having the injection of contrast dye since my veins are small and hard to find. They said I did not need any injections this time, which came as a great relief.

The scan itself was not painful. However, trying to lie still for over an hour was, I was in a lot of pain in my back. The pain in my back is so bad at the moment that I have been taking my ketamine of a night, it helps with the pain but I feel extremely groggy and spaced out after taking it.

12th August 2013:
My appointment with my spinal doctor Mr Neil Oxborrow went reasonably well.

Because I am getting the pain well above where my rods end in my back Mr Neil Oxborrow felt it best to leave things well alone.

The bone scan showed some activity but was inconclusive and again this was not in the place where I am getting most the pain. I do get pain lower down but it's not as bad as it is further up and as I mentioned to my mum I think the discomfort I am getting lower down by my bra strap is due to a small tumour in that area. My mum asked me why I had not told Mr Neil Oxborrow about the discomfort that I get lower down, I think it's because it's more of a really bad throbbing ache rather than a pain.

My mum mentioned to Mr Neil Oxborrow, that Stephen (my orthotic guy) wanted to try mc with a new back brace that he felt would help me more and that he was going to email him about it. Mr Neil Oxborrow said he gets so many emails about braces and that if Stephen felt it would help then he could go ahead and try it, he does not want me to wear the back brace all the time, only when the pain is really bad, which is what I do now anyway. I asked Mr Neil Oxborrow if we could have new picture taken together, which he agreed to do.

Mr Neil Oxborrow and Me

Mr Neil Oxborrow wants me to try doing some Pilates exercise. Pilates is an exercise system that focuses on slow and controlled exercises to help keep muscles toned, flexible and strong. By stretching and strengthening the whole body to improve balance.

I have got my first class booked and will give anything a go if it helps with this pain. We did ask Mr Neil Oxborrow to give us a demonstration but he just laughed.

September 2013:
I have got to have a scan on my stomach, the doctors are unsure if any of the tumours have grown or if any new tumours have grown. My Gastroparisis keeps flaring up and I have not been able to keep fluids down.

I go in hospital in November to have six tumours removed, which is causing a lot of pain and discomfort. If everything goes to plan I will only be in hospital overnight.

28th November 2013:
I had surgery today in which several tumours were removed due to them causing lots of pain and discomfort. My mum came with me, which I really appreciated.

On the morning of my surgery I mentioned to Mr Christopher Duff (my surgeon) that a new tumour had grown in my thigh, and when he looked at it he said its best to have it removed due to how quickly it had grown. After surgery Mr Christopher Duff came to see me and explained that the tumour in my thigh had several tumours growing on top of each other and had started to grow into the muscle. The tumours that were removed in my neck were like a bunch of grapes, but he managed to remove them all.

4th December 2013:
I had my wounds looked at, some had to be redressed, but they were healing well. The scare on my leg is much bigger than I thought it would be (5inc plus) and the same with the scar on my neck, but I suppose the surgeon only went as big as he needed to.

10th December 2013:
My back and knee braces were looked at again this morning; everything went well with this appointment. I

explained that I could not wear my back brace at the moment as the straps go over my shoulder and rub where I have had surgery. He was cool with this and said to wear it when I can.

Mum and I have been asked if we will help with the year 5 OSCE Examinations on the 15th January. I have done this many times in the past and I really enjoy helping the doctors in this way and it also helps the new doctors to understand more about NF. I have been getting so much pain in my back, the pain meds have not really been helping me.

2014

January 2014:

Not a good start for the year my gran (my mum's mum), who I love so much had a fall and ended up in hospital, she also had a mini stroke. Gran was in hospital for ten days and then transferred to a rehabilitation unit for three weeks before being allowed back home. My gran continues to be very confused, but doing well.

I saw Mr Christopher Duff (my plastic surgeon), he is going to remove some more tumours that are giving me some pain. The tumour I had removed in my leg was on the large size and deeper than he first thought, having this tumour removed has left me with a numb part in my leg, and I will not get the full feeling back in this leg now, but it's the risk I take when I have this kind of surgery as the surgeon is dealing with nerve endings and there is always a risk of nerve damage.

My mum was in hospital this month for surgery by Mr Christopher Duff; she had eleven tumours removed. One of the tumours that was removed from my mum's chest got infected and she needed antibiotics.

February 2014:
My mum had a few hospital visits this month, seeing Dr Montague over her prolapsed bladder, and her orthotic doctor for new braces to her knees and hands. Mum also had a brain scan and spine scan done.

The pain in my back has been really bad and I have had a few flair ups with my sickness. I saw Dr Watts who gave me the results of the scan that I had done on my tummy. The scan showed that I have lots of tumours in my tummy along with lots of fluid. I was put on a new tablet called "Ondansetron 4mg"; this medication is given to people who suffer from Gastroparsis. The fluid that showed up on my scan confirmed that I have a severe form of Gastroparsis. The doctor is also writing a letter to my employer to give them some information about the condition.

Sometimes when I am sick I feel much better after it and can continue with my work, but my boss always wants to send me home when I don't need to go home, so the doctor is going to explain this to her.

The doctor is also going to write a new letter for me to take to the A&E department for when my sickness gets really bad as I feel daft going to the hospital just for being sick, but my doctor said it's really important that I do go to A&E for IV treatment.

I am at the pain clinic in April as I am in so much pain with my back. I am still in a back brace when the pain is really bad, but it does not always help.

April 2014:
I had a lovely birthday with family and friends with lots of lovely surprises on the day.

More hospital visits and the dentist; too much chocolate and cake, I guess, I need a filling waaa! I will have the filling in a few weeks' time. I have booked the dentist appointment on the same day as another hospital appointment so that I am not missing too much work.

I have been to physio regarding my back and legs and as it stands the physio won't look into the pain in my legs, they are only willing to do the physio on the top of my back and told me I needed acupuncture; they felt that I would benefit from this treatment. I have told them I don't think I can do this due to the needles and would not be able to relax while they did it. I have spoken to my GP regarding this and she is referring me back to my knee specialist to see if he can help.

Regarding the pain in my back, I am going to try some different posture movements. The pain in my back is getting worse.

I am seeing my pain specialist this week (Dr Lierberman), fingers crossed he comes up with some answers for me. I know if he can help, he will, as he is such a nice guy. I am also due to see my NF doctor (Dr Sue Huson) who again will help me if she can.

I went back to see one of my GP's last week as I had to let her know how I was getting on with the new tablets that I had been given by Dr Watts (my Gastro doctor) for my Gastroparesis (Ondemet 4mg), which I have had to take one of three times a day. Unfortunately, the tablets have not really helped with my sickness. I still kept being sick when I took the tablets, I did not see the point in continuing to take them, so I have now stopped and my sickness is still the same.

Gastroparesis is a lifelong condition; living with this condition not only affects the person living with it, but also affects family and friends. I think it affects my friends and I a lot because we struggle to go out for meals sometimes because I might end up having to leave the table suddenly due to being sick. I haven't been able to eat a proper meal in the past few weeks without throwing up. I have been dealing with this condition for a few years now, I would like to say it gets better, but it does not. I do have good days and I have bad days, and in work it can be irritating because people think I have a bug and trying to explain that I am not sick because of having a bug, I'm sick due to a condition that I have is hard for them to understand sometimes.

Gastroparesis is also called delayed gastric emptying. The term "gastric" refers to the stomach. Normally, your stomach empties its contents in a controlled manner into your small intestines. In gastroparesis, the muscles that contract and move your food along the digestive tract don't work properly so your stomach empties too slowly.

It takes skill and strength to deal with this challenging digestive condition. It means always looking for what does and does not help your sickness. I have pretty much stopped taking milk as I think it irritates my stomach a lot, so the only milk I get is through cheese – and if and when I have a chocolate milkshake from McDonalds, when I do though, I am sick. It's catch 22 situation.

Well, that it's from me for now, but please remember:
I'm here as a support for you, to be a friend, someone you can sound off at when you're feeling down. If you need any advice or just want somewhere you can meet fellow sufferers then please contact me!

While people of any age struggle to adjust to a life with pain it can be particularly hard for teenagers and those in their early 20s. At a time when the world should be opening up, offering exciting things, it can feel as if a door has slammed shut instead. Don't dwell on what you can't do, but concentrate on what you can, explore new interests and you will be amazed at how much it helps.

Anyone can tell you it won't hurt tomorrow. But I'm here to listen while it hurts today.

I intend to take each day as it comes and appreciate what life has given me, because that is what life is all about.

Stories from other People who have NF

Although NF is a wide-ranging disorder, each of us who have NF shares a common bond. NF does not necessarily bring each of us severe complications, but it does bring each of us a measure of uncertainty. No doctor can tell you how your NF will affect you, because they don't know. NF is different for everyone, as you will read while reading all different stories. The sharing of information and support can be valuable. Each one of us has a unique life experience in living with NF, which we may find beneficial to share.

My Mum (Julie) and Me

I was born 54 years ago with neurofibromatosis (NF1), which the doctors didn't know at the time. I was ten years old before I was given the official NF1 diagnoses.

I had been getting a lot of pain in my side and mentioned it to my mum; there was a small lump in the area that I was getting the pain so my mum took me to the doctors. The doctor did not seem too concerned at the time and then he asked my mum if I had any brown marks on my body and my mum said that I had loads on my back. The doctor asked if he could have a look at them, it was at this point the doctor looked shocked and said that he would be writing to the hospital. He mentioned to my mum that I might have a condition called "Von Recklinghausen" (back in the 60s this is what they called NF) and then asked if anyone in the family had the condition.

No one on my mum's side had the condition so my mum contacted my dad (who she had divorced when I was only a baby) to ask him if he had a condition called

Von Recklinghausen, he said there was nothing wrong with him and refused to help the doctors. I remember seeing him when I was about three years old and he had lots of lumps on his head then. I am 100% sure my dad had NF1.

I went into hospital a couple of weeks later to have the lump removed and to have a biopsy done on the lump. It was confirmed I had NF1. Every time I went to the hospital I would have loads of doctors coming in to see me; I was not sure what was going on, I just thought it was normal.

I had no real health problems growing up, but I did struggle in school with spelling and grammar; I hated reading out aloud in class as I always found it difficult to do this in front of other people.

When I was younger not a lot was known about NF1, I was told in class I did not pay attention, which I did.

When I left school I worked in a nursery. I had my own group of ten children to care for; I loved my job and stayed for over twelve years.

I married a wonderful man (John) in August 1985 and my first child (Christopher) was born in September 1986.

I was told I could not have children due to having polycystic ovaries, so when Christopher was born I was over the moon. I was warned that he could have NF1 and that any children I do have was at 50% risk of having NF1.

After Christopher was born I left my job as a nursery nurse and worked two nights a week on the children's ward at my local hospital – that way I could be with Christopher in the day and John would be home in the evening for him. Again, I loved caring for the children and helping them get better, some nights were upsetting on the ward for obvious reasons.

After two years working at the hospital I started to have health problems myself and had to leave my job.

Christopher was two years old by now and still showed no signs of having NF1. He was such a lovely child. I never had any issues with Christopher; out of nappies in the day by twelve months old, walking at eleven months old and out of nappies by 16 months of a night. He never cried when I put him to bed of a night, he was such a happy child.

Then in April 1990, my beautiful daughter (Kirsty) was born. At first Kirsty looked perfect. Then when I went to bath her in the hospital I saw the sign of NF1: those dreaded brown birth marks on her back and one very small tumour. I mentioned it to the doctor on his ward round, but I was told it is far too early to say she has NF, but I knew different and at eleven weeks old Kirsty was diagnosed with NF1. I was not worried by this news, as I had been OK growing up with the condition, I was never told much about the condition when I was growing up, I never saw doctors about my condition. I never knew the problems NF could cause. So much more is now known about NF than when I first found out I had the condition back in the 60s. To be honest NF was just a word to me; I did not know the condition could be so scary and that it could cause internal tumours.

Kirsty was on target with all her health checks when growing up. Like her brother, Kirsty was out of nappies in the day by the time she was twelve months, walking by twelve months and out of nappies at night by sixteen months. Kirsty use to model for Tuesdays Child, everyone loved her on set; she would shout "POT", which meant she wanted her potty. You can see some of her modeling pictures on her web page.

Kirsty's NF has given her so many problems, as you will read from her story.

My health issues are mainly due to me having arthritis in my knees, top of spine, shoulder and fingers. I do have high blood pressure but it's not sure if it's due to my NF. I have a very mild scoliosis but I have never seen anybody for it. The pain in my back and shoulder is so bad that it wakes me up every night. I walk with the aid of crutches and have to wear braces on both my knees as they give way on me; I have ended up on the floor so many times. I also wear braces on both my hands to help support my wrists.

Over the past few months the pain in my left shoulder and top of my back has been getting worse. I also keep getting numbness in my little finger and ring fingers on my left hand, this tends to happen more when my elbow is bent or is resting on the chair arm. I also keep getting muscle jerks in my legs and arms this again is when I am resting. I am not sure if these sensations are due to my NF or not. I have recently been told that I have brisk reflexes and that I may also have stiff leg syndrome, which is another nerve related condition.

I have had lots of the NF tumours removed over the years due to the tumours giving me so much pain and when they have grown in awkward place. I am going into hospital later in the year to have about eight tumours removed due to them giving me pain and discomfort, some of the tumours I am having removed are on the sole of my foot and are very sore when I walk.

I do have the Lisch nodules: tiny, noncancerous tumors on my iris (the coloured part of my eyes). These nodules have nothing to do with my reduced vision. But for people who have these nodules they can help to confirm a diagnosis of NF.

Living with NF can be very scary, but I am surrounded by so many people who love and support me, it makes dealing with NF much easier. There are things I might have had to work harder at, for example, in school and when I was able to work, and there are some physical things that are more difficult because of my pain but I will never give in to NF. You only have one life and I intend to live it.

We know NF can be cruel, that's plain and simple. However, Kirsty inherited more than just NF1 from me. Kirsty's got the fighting spirit; the loving heart and a passion that will never let her give up! She loves life and helping others.

It is a very personal choice whether or not to have children when you know you have a condition that can be passed on. There is no right answer. We all have to do what we think is right in our hearts. For me I could not imagine life without my two beautiful children.

By: Julie Ashton

My Story Elli

My name is Carly Jim, and I am mummy to a wonderful little girl called Ellie who was diagnosed with neurofibromatosis 1 when she was only five months old. When Ellie was first diagnosed without a doubt the thing that most helped me accept the condition and think about Ellie's future in a positive way was reading Kirsty's Story. I came away from reading Kirsty's Story thinking wow having NF doesn't have to hold you back, in fact it can be the source of your fighting spirit and that whilst there may be tough times and sad times in between these you can have some amazing experiences. If my little Ellie grows up to be even a tiny bit like Kirsty then I will be a very proud mummy indeed. But enough about me, what I would like to do is to try my best to tell you about Ellie in the way that she would describe herself if she was able to type, so this is Ellie's story so far – as ghost written by mummy woo woo (that's a bad impression of me being a ghost, my husband would groan).

OK here goes – My name is Ellie Jim, not just Ellie (or even Elizabeth as it says on my birth certificate); if you ask me I will say 'Ellie Jim' with a big smile because I am proud not only of my name but also the fact that I can now say it because although I am three years old now until very recently I said very few words at all. When I did decide to start talking I skipped the middle bit and went straight to talking in full sentences and I am now very chatty. My leaders at play group said to my mummy that whilst they are impressed at how much I have come on now that I am talking they can hear me being a bit bossy to the other children, oops, but yes I am a bit bossy, especially with Daddy, but in a way it is a good thing because although I am teeny tiny (if you were to get one hundred kids my age and line them up from smallest to largest I would be the second smallest) I am large in stature and I would never let anyone push me around because of my size. I am what Mummy refers to as 'spunky' and I would agree with that; I know my own mind, what I like and what I don't like, and at the moment top of my list of likes are orange juice, milk, ice cream, crisps, Mickey and Minnie Mouse and of course all the Disney princesses. Although I am a bit bossy I am very caring and look after everybody, especially my older brother Danny and my best friend Freddie.

Mummy says that I have something called NF and I know that I see doctors, some doctors I like, especially when they give me stickers, and some doctors I don't like but I am always a good girl and let them examine me. I don't like the x-ray machine very much but Mummy and Daddy give me lots of treats like crisps and chocolate when I have to visit the doctors. One doctor gave me vitamin drops which I have every day, I like my drops and I say "the doctor gave them to me for my bones". Mummy tells me that I am special, and she calls me a princess, I say "I am a princess if I got my princess dress on but not if I not got my dress on". Sometimes a man comes to the house to take pictures and I say "cheese" I like saying cheese and I like posing for photos, I get very excited when I see myself in the paper raising awareness of NF, I point and say "that's me Ellie Jim". in fact one day when I wasn't in the paper I was grumpy and said "Ellie Jim not there".

Although I have this genetic condition I am not a sickly child, and for the most part you wouldn't know that I was any different to anyone else, that is as long as I am fully dressed, once you take my clothes off you can see that I have a poorly chest, it dips in and I have lots of brown marks too. Mummy says the doctor will mend my dip when I am bigger. So far the most noticeable way the NF has affected me is that I have a large tumour in my left leg, it goes from the ankle up to the knee and is making my leg longer and wider than the other one, and because of the leg I get unbalanced and fall over a lot. I also tend to skip when I walk which does look super cute but my legs do get tired easily if I dance or jump or even just walk. Mummy likes to encourage me to walk to build up my strength but she does a lot of cuddling me too (so does Daddy) I don't mind though because I like cuddles and I like being really high up, which I am not normally because I am so tiny. The doctor who looks at my leg says I will have to have an operation when I am older, for now I am just trying to ignore it and try not to fall splat on my face too much. I am starting kindergarten in September and I am super excited because "I am a big girl now". Mummy says that I am her magic wand and that I was given to her because I am special and because she is in a position to help other people with NF, I love my mummy, and she loves me too, and Mummy says she will always do her best to make the world a better place for me and all my friends.

By: Carly Jim

My Story By: John

I am John, from Glasgow, Scotland. The first symptoms of Neurofibromatosis appeared when I was only two. My parents found a lump on the outside of my right ankle. My doctor referred me to an orthopedic surgeon. After several years of treatment he told my parents that the best solution was amputation, my parents where against this.

One day when my mother came to pick me up from school she saw me struggling to protect my leg from older boys playing football (soccer), due to the fact the slightest bump would leave me in agony. After seeing this, my parents decided that amputation might after all be the best option. When we went back to the surgeon he said he would put us on to another surgeon at a different hospital to see if he could do anything for me.

I had three operations at this hospital. The third surgery was to remove the tumor and it was this surgeon who diagnosed Neurofibromatosis, by which time I was seven years old. He was against amputation on young children under the age of 12 years because it would have meant that I would have to have kept going back for operations every few years to have bone growth cut as I was growing. The operations on my ankle left my ankle very badly disfigured and discoloured. I had a scar from the thigh down to my ankle. At school I was unable to take part in any contact sports like soccer. My teachers took pity on me and gave me extra swimming classes. I continued to go back to the hospital for six monthly checkups.

When I was 18 another tumor appeared behind my knee on the same leg. Two biopsies were taking to determine if the tumor was malignant. Deep down I knew that I was going to lose my leg and with the problems I had with it for most of my life it was my preferred option. When the dressing was removed to take out my stitches I was shocked at the state of my wound. Blood and yellow liquid, which I assumed was the tumor, was oozing from the wound. When I saw that I then knew that is was not going to be saved and nor did I want it to be. A second biopsy was taken. It was a couple of long and anxious before weeks before I was finally given the result that I already knew; my leg was going to be amputated. At first they did not know just how much would be taken off but in the end they thought it better to amputate from the hip. I had my leg amputated on November 8 1978.

It was over 24 years before my next surgery. I was having problems emptying my bowels. After a rather unpleasant examination of my back passage my doctor suspected neurofroma. An MRI scan confirmed this and also showed the lump was on my right buttock (amputee side). I had a biopsy, which showed the tumor to be low-grade malignancy. I had to have a long operation. I had this operation on the 24 January 2003. I had two surgeons – one orthopaedic to remove the lump from my side, and another to remove it from my bowel. There was a lot of nerve damage and I have lost some feeling on my right side and have a little difficulty in empting my bowels. I will continue to have regular CT Scans for probably life.

So far, after ten years it hasn't returned.

I had educational problems. I found it difficult concentrating and following instructions. Even now my concentration is still quite poor. It wasn't until I began to read about the effects of NF that I thought my educational problems may have been down it.

No one else anywhere in my family has Neurofibromatosis.

By: John Cassidy

My Story By: Cassie

NF never really affected me until I was 15; mine was more or less a skin problem rather than medical. Mine all started off with slight back pain when I was at school and I thought nothing of it, by the time I was 18 the pain had moved to my knees. I kept going to and from the doctors and was just told to exercise more or that I didn't look in pain (that helped lol). It was when I was 20 I saw my old NF doctor, who actually laughed at me and said NF doesn't cause pain, and by this time I was in agony and struggling to walk, I wasn't going to give up though as I knew deep down something wasn't right. I got some help from a woman in the USA called Gail, she is in a wheelchair due to Nf, she wrote a two page letter and spoke to doctors in the USA who told me to contact the Neuro Foundation. I contacted them within minutes and the lady on the other line wasn't happy that I had been left. Within weeks I had an NF professor, Professor Charles French, and an NF nurse Marie Mcgill. I was happy that finally I was going to get help, but it was when I went to see the professor that I found out NF wasn't just a skin condition. He said he could feel a tumour so sent me for scans, he found multiple tumours and lumbars 1 2 3 4 5; one of which is causing a disc to bulge. I also suffer from scoliosis which gives some terrible neck and back pain, it's like a vicious circle, I started to search the net for books which is where I found Kirsty's book, it has been the BIGGEST help EVER!! Kirsty and her mum Julie have been great and are now two very good friends of mine, like Kirsty I use an elbow crutch to get around. When I am really bad I use my wheelchair. NF has cost me friends and more upsetting my dream job of being a police officer.

I am having pain management which I am hoping can help and I'm awaiting a profiling bed to help me turn and get up from a lying down position as I find turning in bed difficult at times due to when the pain is at its worst. My GP found a tumour about the size of a small satsuma growing in my tummy which will probably need removing as it's already giving me pain.
I recently found out I have tumours attached to nearly all the nerves in my right leg and the pain is pretty bad.

I am now hoping to do some home courses; one which includes English as my punctuation is terrible and my spelling is not too great.

By: Cassie Gunn

My Story By: Simon

I often say that I don't have Neurofibromatosis, but neurofibromatosis has me and I'm far more obnoxious and annoying than neurofibromatosis can ever be. And it's true, I am, just ask my girlfriend.

I know it's probably not appropriate but I tend not to take my neurofibromatosis too seriously. Yes it's a debilitating, sometimes painful condition to live with, it's also left me with a kypho-scoliosis that has required a lot of surgery to not correct very well, I have fibromas that are sometimes disfiguring and yes, I'm one of those really annoying people that names them, and they all have their own stories and one day when I'm bored they will probably even gain their own personalities and I'll write a rather inappropriate and insane soap opera about them, but I digress, I'm here to say what my neurofibromatosis means to me.

Has it defined who I am? As much as I'd like to say no, it most certainly has. Teamed up with my dad, who also has neurofibromatosis, we both fail to see why life should be serious; we laugh about it, make jokes about it and make quite a fine double act due to it, the only thing is he has cooler scars than me, but I have cooler hair. Yeah, I've digressed again…

So, what can I say about my neurofibromatosis experiences? Well, I have been bullied for it, I've had people point and stare at the funny man, it's left me short in stature and it has left me disabled, I have all the lumps, bumps, scars and interesting freckles and spots neurofibromatosis so generously likes to give, but I refuse point blank to let that stop me doing what I want. I present radio shows online, I produce graphic art, play guitar in a rock band and produce electronic music. I've even been a death metal vocalist. So, despite my neurofibromatosis I've made sure I've had a fun life and I've made sure I've not let it beat me.

I know physically neurofibromatosis has treated me badly, I also know that as it progresses my condition could get worse and I may throw away my walking stick and replace it with a wheelchair, but I'm fine with that, I've accepted it, even embraced the neurofibromatosis to a degree. It's a part of who I am, and I like me. I like me a lot. So I wouldn't change it for all the tea in China. And I like tea too, a lot.

So, back to the original point… What does having neurofibromatosis mean to me?

I don't have neurofibromatosis. Neurofibromatosis has me, and as my girlfriend will surely testify, I'm far more obnoxious, and annoying than it will ever be. And I like it that way.

By: Simon Maslak

My Story By: Aaron

I was about six or seven when I found out that I had nf1 with one leg shorter than the other; I have a plexiform neurofibroma in my left calf, and other little bumps and café au lait marks dotted about. I attended Great Ormond street hospital in London where I had two operations to correct the length difference between the two legs, (Dr Hill).

School was hard, I did get slightly bullied, but one thing I learnt was never react or else they would continue – once they realise it doesn't bother you, they leave you alone.

I have never let it stop me from doing anything; I've always been an active person. I went to the Kent Mountain Centre in Llanberis, Snowdonia national park, (it's an outdoors centre), and whilst kayaking there the instructor pulled me aside and asked if I had considered doing my 1 star kayaking exam (I didn't know it existed), so I did it and passed, during the next four years I clocked up my 2, 3 star certificates and started training to become an instructor.

I left school at 16 and went to Thanet College in 2005 on a professional catering NVQ level 1 course. I did NVQ 2 and 3 as well, and whilst at college I did work experience at Buckingham Palace and Windsor castle, highlight being the French state visit in 2008 absolutely FANASTIC!

Whilst at college on spare days, I worked at Eastwell Manor, Ashford under the watchful eye of Neil Wiggins, a person I must thank for helping train me to get me to where I am today.

In last months at college, we had a visit from Gary Lambert, Head of HR at Big Cedar lodge, south west Missouri, America. I would be lying if I said I didn't leap off my chair at a chance to go there. Anyway, an interview later and a stressful trip to the US embassy in London and I was on a plane heading across the pond. As I got off the plane it hit me 'I was going to be working at a top American resort, yes me!' It was kind of hard to start off, but I settled in, a year shot past, my parents came over for two weeks (their first time to America), we went on a mini road trip through some of the southern states all I will say is WOW!

I have had a couple of chef's jobs since returning but have settled at a restaurant in Winchelsea Bay, East Sussex where I am Head Chef.

December 2012 I was seen by Dr Guy Leschziner at Guy's Hospital, at the specialist neurofibromatosis clinic, where I had a full examination and was sent for a PET scan and MRI scan to see if anything can be done, well that's my story so far.

I guess all I have to say now is never let NF stop you from doing anything, and remember you have NF not the other way round.

By Aaron Woodhams

My Story By: Luke

I was first diagnosed with NF1 at the age of five by my GP, from birth I did have the common signs of NF, the freckling of the armpits and the café-au-lait spots on my body. My right leg was also shorter than my right by about an inch.

Throughout primary school I was seeing a specialist in Taunton about trying to correct the length of the shorter leg. The decision was to wait until I was twelve before they would perform the correction procedure.

The idea of the operation was to slow the growth of my longer leg to allow the shorter one to catch up. To do this the surgeon decided to remove bone from both the femur and tibia from behind the knee. By scrapping the bone he hoped to remove enough bone growth to sufficiently stunt its growth. I had my leg in plaster for about seven weeks and the doctor thought it would take about three years for the legs to equalise in length. By the time I was eighteen I noticed that my short leg was now in fact longer than the other by about an inch. I now have a built up shoe for the other foot.

The next time I was in hospital was when I was fourteen. I discovered a large neurofibroma on my lower back, so I returned to see the surgeon who had performed the procedure on my knee and he decided to perform another operation. So a few months later I went in to the Nuffield Hospital in Taunton to undergo the new procedure. It turns out that the neurofibroma was the size of two adult fists, and I left after a few days in hospital.

I had to return a few days later with a massive amount of bleeding around the site of the removal of the neurofibroma. I went back into surgery to find the location of the bleeding, but I continued to bleed after that operation. My GP referred me to Frenchay Hospital in Bristol. After another operation they successfully manage to stop the bleeding.

When I was sixteen, myself and my family began to notice that my spine was beginning to curve, so we made another appointment to see the spinal surgeon at Frenchay. After numerous x-rays the doctor there thought it was too dangerous to operate on. Thank God my family was not put off by this news, because they wrote to hundreds of hospitals around the UK asking if anyone would be willing to take on my case.

The only hospital to respond was the John Radcliff in Oxford and Dr Sue Huson and a Mr. Fairbanks an Orthopaedic Surgeon agreed to see me. It had been eighteen months of searching for someone to review my case. So my family and I went to Oxford to see them and I had more x-rays, including CT scans and a MRI scan. After reviewing all the tests Mr. Fairbanks decided to take on my case and proposed a course of action. The spine was too severe to straighten so he decided the best thing to do was to stop it from getting any worse. The plan was to take the fibula from my right leg and graft it on to the spine.

The operation lasted for thirteen hours and I spent seven days in the intensive care unit. I was taken to the ward to recuperate and after getting over the effects of the anaesthetic I was gradually asked to get mobile.

Unfortunately in doing so it caused the bone graft to separate from the spine, and I was quickly rushed back into theatre where they reattached the fibula and for security added a metal rod. The second operation lasted about ten hours and I spent another five days in intensive care.

This time after the operation I was told that I would be bed bound for six months and I stayed in Oxford for another month after to get myself ready for the ambulance journey back to my parents. I then spent the next six months confined to bed in the lounge at my parents and not being allowed to sit up. As I started to feel better I decided to continue my studies from my bed and my teacher from college came a few times to give me coursework. After the six months was up the decision was made that that I should start intensive four-week course of both physiotherapy and aqua therapy at Musgrove Park Hospital. It must have been another two months before I was mobile and getting around again on my own.

Since then I have regular checkups in Oxford, with occasional MRI's just to ensure everything is still all right. I had to have some plexi-form neurofibromas removed from my lower back and right thigh, as they were getting uncomfortable. Unfortunately the plexi-form neurofibromas have grown back.

After a PET scan in 2008 they noticed some neurofibromas in my lower back which they were concerned about, because they were showing signs that they could be cancerous. I again went into theatre and proceeded to have these removed. They also found several others that did not show up on the scan. The results came back and luckily they were all benign. This was the last operation I had.

Even with all the hurdles of my NF, I finished college, went to
university and completed a degree and now have a good job doing what I like. I do now have to walk with crutches as I have problems walking any distance and find standing for any amount of time difficult, but on the plus side without the spinal operation I would have almost certainly ended up in a wheelchair, and I have always said that the NF has made me the person I am today and I am happy with that.

By Luke Farnham

My Story By: Lisa

I was diagnosed with Neurofibromatosis Type 1 and ADHD, when I was 15. I was at boarding school at the time and was taken out on various occasions to see specialists.

My relationship with my parents was never the best. I was adopted at birth, so unsure if my NF was a spontaneous mutation or if one on my biological parents was affected. I have never attempted to look for my biological parents either and have no wish to. My mother sent me to boarding school because I was a bit of a rebel and she found she could not cope when my father was away working.

We now have a better relationship but not as I would like. I think this also played a part in my not accepting I had NF. I remember being taken to all the doctors and then my mother just producing a medication and not explaining what it was for, but insisting I took it. There was also an incident where she basically told me that because I had NF, I wasn't what she wanted to adopt; she wanted a healthy child, not a broken one, because I was costing her a fortune in medical bills.

Anyway, I have basically ignored my NF since. I moved out of home aged 16, I am now 32. I am one of the luckier ones, as have little visible external tumours but quite a lot of café-au-lait marks. It's now been discovered I have a tumour on the brain stem, fortunately non-cancerous and my back is a little wonky. I suffer from constant, persistent migraines, moderate back pain and leg pain. I have terrible balance and have been accused of being 'drunk' to people that don't know me or the fact that I have NF1. I only recently, like in the last 18 months, found all the amazing groups on the internet and have a large NF family now and have found someone in my hometown that has NF also. Although I was ignoring my NF, I was aware I always had it and always felt very alone, probably why I tried to ignore it. Now I have found the groups and other people with it, I can link a lot of what I have up to my NF and it doesn't seem as bad. I have had to accept that certain activities I used to enjoy aggravate my NF, such as jumping on quad bikes which makes things hurt, or roller coasters at theme parks which affect my balance and cause migraines, playing rugby also had to be stopped because being tackled began to hurt more than it should. Saying that, I will still do these activities, but only in moderation. I refuse to stop living my life and having fun because of a medical condition.

By Lisa Presley.

My Story By: Jo

I was born late into the night in April 1979, the second child to my parents, my brother, Anthony being born two years before. My family discovered I had NF following a routine home visit from my brother's consultant. He saw my brother, me and my mum altogether and immediately knew what was causing all these problems. NF has affected my family in a huge way, but I refuse to let it beat me.

I first began having problems with my left leg when I was around 12 months old and beginning to learn to walk. Unknown to my parents at the time, the bones in my lower left leg hadn't formed as they should, so, when I tried to walk, my leg simply gave way. My parents took me to York District Hospital A&E department, where I was x-rayed, and probably prodded and poked for a few hours! It was then that it was discovered my leg had broken. My parents were interviewed separately, and asked how I came to break my leg in such a way… was my dad rough with me?

Did my mum ever lose her temper with me? It wasn't until afterwards, when we were allowed home that they realised the enormity of the situation; I had broken my leg, and initially, my parents were under suspicion of causing the break!

After many follow-up visits, my leg still was not healing, and so I was referred to another hospital. They were unable to help, so I was sent back to York, who then sent me to Sheffield. After weeks of waiting, my parents hadn't heard anything, so took me back to York to demand something be done. My parents were given three options. (one: send me to Edinburgh Children's Hospital or two: send me to Great Ormond Street Hospital (GOSH) in London). My parents dared to ask the consultant what the third option was; "amputation" he said. Thankfully, they chose to send me to GOSH! I spent the next eight or nine years traveling backwards and forwards from our home in York to London, having around five operations. It came to the point where GOSH were unable to help any further, so was referred again. This time to one of the best orthopaedic surgeons at the time, in St Peter's Hospital in Chertsey, and also St Thomas' in London.

I had a bone graft at St Thomas' when I was about nine or ten, where they removed a section of my right fibula and put it in my left leg, to replace the metal pin. After my first checkup, about six weeks after surgery, the consultant said I could start to gradually weight-bare, so, the next day at school, I threw a football down the playing field, chasing after it on my crutches. As I went to kick the ball, I lost my balance and fell in a crumpled heap with my legs tangled around my crutches. My dad was called and I was whisked away to A&E where we found out I had now fractured my femur! Oops!

My last operation on my leg was after my GCSEs – whilst all my friends were enjoying their summer break, I was in hospital having major surgery. I had an Illazarov fixator to lengthen my left leg by around 1½ inches, and spent the next six months turning the screws to stretch my bone apart.

My brother, Anthony, had his own problems with NF too. He had an optic glioma on one of his nerves, in addition to hydrocephalus. He didn't have too many great problems with the tumour, but had a shunt fitted to help drain some of the fluid caused by hydrocephalus. He led a normal life, and had some fantastic friends. Six weeks into his college course, where he hoped to learn to become a chef, he died very suddenly and unexpectedly in his sleep. He was 16, I was 14. Nothing prepared us for it, and no-one saw it coming. The post mortem listed a long list of things; the tumour being one of the contributing factors.

At 21, I became a parent myself, though by the time my son was born, I was a single parent and faced with the prospect of raising my son alone, though my parents and friends were fantastic and a real support. In late July 2000, I gave birth to Reece Anthony, a healthy 8lb 8oz bundle of joy. It was realised he had NF soon after birth, and so began having regular checkups with a paediatrician.

In 2004, when Reece was 3½ our family was hit with the next bombshell. Reece was diagnosed with Rhabdomyosarcoma, a form of cancer, which had hit his muscle tissue around his bladder and kidneys. When they discovered the tumour, it was the size of a tennis ball. After nine sessions of chemotherapy, and surgery to remove part of the tumour, Reece was "free" of cancer. He is now 13, and almost nine years since he finished treatment. He now has minor problems with his kidneys and some minor learning issues, and has a growth hormone deficiency. They aren't sure if this is caused by NF or by one of the types of chemo he had, as both can cause it. He currently had daily injections to help his growth

As for me, I met a wonderful man in 2010, he moved in within three weeks, and three weeks after moving in he proposed while at York Races. We married in 2012, and Reece was best man for Simon. I didn't forget my brother on my big day though. Between the ceremony and the meal, I took my bouquet to the cemetery to put on my brother's grave.

I may have NF, and be limited as to what I can and can't do, but I refuse to be beaten by it. I have NF, it doesn't have me.

By: Jo Arundel

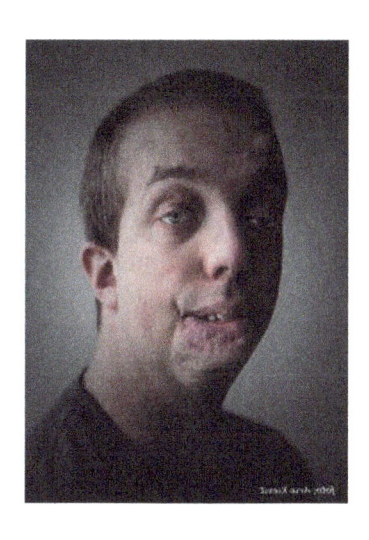

My Story By: David

My name is David Oosterloo and I have Neurofibromatosis type 1, I'm 25 years old and I live in The Netherlands. I have had NF since the moment I was born, because I inherited it from my dad.

I always knew I had NF1, and I think it helped me to accept NF and my facial anomaly I have because of NF. Currently I have seven or eight neurofibromas. Two of them are on my face, one of them on my forehead and the other one is on my chin, on the left under the lip. Because of this I have a big lip. It makes me look different, but it doesn't mean I am different, I believe that beauty comes from within. My biggest neurofibroma is on my elbow. It is a size of an egg. Another big one is on the back of my head. The rest of my neurofibromas are very small and they are spread over my body.

Because of NF I also have scoliosis. This is a curvature of the spine.

In the beginning I had physiotherapy for it, but as time passed surgery was needed. I had surgery in 2002 in a hospital in Belgium. They took some pieces of bone from the protruding parts of my spine, they grinded these pieces of bone to make new bones. They used these bones to support the irons pins they use to secure my spine. I used morphine for pain for three days, but didn't use any pain medication after that. I had to stay in the hospital for 14 days, and went home in an Ambulance after that. I was very happy I could go home lying down, as I couldn't sit straight up for an long time so a drive home would have been an nightmare.

I also have Lisch nodules and hanging eyelids. I have difficulties seeing object that are far away. As an example, a plane in the sky, it takes me more time to spot it and sometimes I won't spot it at all. I can also have difficulties with color contrasts, some colors together make it difficult for me to read a text.

Unfortunately I suffer from hyperventilation and panic attacks as well. Because of that I have depression and I still suffer social isolation. I didn't dare to leave my bedroom for five to eight months. It was an very hard period because I had to leave my job. At the same moment I had a possibly new job coming up, I had to leave there as well. Luckily I dared to leave my room, our house and sometimes our city. It took me a few years because I had to do it step by step. I had to regain my confidence. It was like a psychological game. Fear for fear that turned into fear, I had to teach myself not to be afraid. I had some psychological help for that and I still have today.

The problems I still have today are appointments, being in a place at a specific time gives me a lot of tension. I'm trying to work on that, and I believe I can overcome that as well.

A few years ago I made my own website about NF; I wanted to make a website where I can tell my friends, classmates and teachers about NF in my own words. During the years I wanted to make NF more known in The Netherlands and recently I want to make it world known. I try to connect with people and work together with other people who have the same goals. See my website at www.watisnf.nl

Enough about my disorder now, let me tell you something about myself. I learned to be a sous chef, but unfortunately I couldn't pass my last exams so I had to stop. But I did two thirds of it so I'm a happy person. I would like to work in an institutional kitchen and cook for elderly people. It's really nice work and I would love to do that when I'm able to do so.

Because I have a lot of spare time now, I'm a service and support team member for a forum software company that is used worldwide. I do this volunteer work for the Dutch support website of this software. I am also a patient support advocate for NF Mid-Atlantic, a Neurofibromatosis organization located in the United States. People can email to me to discuss NF and my personal experiences. I really like to help people with NF and make a difference in other's lives. NF can be a hard part of our lives and nobody has to do that fight alone.

Besides doing these important things in my spare time I like to watch movies, play games on my game console, or build Lego models.

I want to close my story with saying this: looking different doesn't mean that someone is different. Don't judge people by how they look. Real beauty comes from within. And, if you are having a hard time because of NF… don't feel alone. Reach out to the NF community, there are some wonderful people out there with NF that are very inspirational. They can't take away your pain or disabilities, but they can make you feel better.

By: David Oosterloo

Katie's NF1 story

It was quite a scary time when my twins, Joseph & Katie, were born at 33 weeks in 2003. Spending six weeks in SCBU was all a bit surreal but we got through it. Life with two tiny babies was exhausting but equally it was so very special. Strangers would often come up to me and tell me how special I was to have boy/girl twins. I always realised how special they were as babies and they are equally special as nine year olds.

I realised early on that Katie was very different to Joseph. Joe put on weight, slept through from 12 weeks and was whilst he was slightly slower at reaching certain milestones than average babies, I never worried about him.

Whilst I didn't know/understand why at the time, Katie was very different. She never slept through the night (she still doesn't), she projectile vomited after every feed, didn't progress onto solids until 18 months and was still in nappies at almost four years.

At six months she developed a large brown tummy mark that, as the months went on, grew bigger, until it covered a large area of her torso. She was also very floppy and bendy. She was seen by a number of specialists from being a baby and for a while we were under the main care of dermatologists for a 'skin complaint'.

In spring 2009, aged five, it became more evident that she had more and more large (some huge) brown marks had appeared on her skin plus she had speech problems. She was finally diagnosed with Neurofibromatosis type 1. I'd never heard of NF1 so I Googled it. It was pretty scary reading.

From then my life totally changed. It became obvious from her first MRI that whist the neurofibroma on her torso was big, the plexiform inside her was huge. She was also diagnosed with scoliosis.

During the past four years Katie has been through so many hospital appointments – she has regular MRIs under general anaesthetic, X-rays, CT scans, PET scans, blood tests, extensive speech therapy etc. Throughout it all she remains a happy, smiley little girl. She knows all her Drs and consultants really well as she sees them often and she asks lots and lots of questions (Dr Sue Huson can testify to this lol). She is not fazed by anything.

Sadly she suffers with chronic pain and is on a lot of medication…luckily a few of her tablets can be crushed and added to her nightly chocolate mousse. She doesn't flinch by all the medicines she merely accepts them She also accepted wearing a brace for 23 hours a day.

Last summer (Sept 2012) she had a large neurofibroma removed from her back as it had grown very quickly was bleeding a lot and so caused concern to the NF nurses and our paediatric surgeon. She spent a week in hospital. At that point I realised that this was likely to be what life would be like…lots of appointments and various operations. However we are lucky as our support and care at the Leeds general Infirmary (LGI) has been, and continues to be amazing.

I would never say that dealing with NF1 (and scoliosis) is easy. There are days when Katie is in too much pain to do much at all and her mobility has been affected greatly. However we are extremely lucky in that we have a supportive network of family and friends who give Katie, myself and Joseph continued care and support in so many different ways.

Katie faces major surgery during summer 2013 as her spine is now curving at 80 degrees and so two surgeons will work together to try and remove a section of the plexiform so that the spine surgeon can insert growing rods, until she is big enough for full spinal fusion. Before then however, Katie may need another operation on her back to remove more of the neurofibroma as its bleeding daily and they cannot carry out the major surgery until her back has healed a bit.

Facing major surgery is difficult for anyone but again both Katie and I ask both surgeons lots of questions. In the end, as a parent, you put your ultimate trust in their abilities.

We also receive fantastic support from the NF team at Manchester, our paediatrician at Bradford and our clinical psychologist. Also regular hydrotherapy helps Katie. Regular support and coffees (and wine) with my friends helps me.

For those reading things thinking that we have a fantastic network of people supporting us, we do. We are lucky that we have regular appointments with two brilliant surgeons who know and understand Katie really well, as do Dr Huson and the NF nurses. We also have a local paediatrician who sees Katie every six months to check her blood pressure, blood test (she has Vit D defiecicancy) and general care. We also have yearly eye tests, see a specialist speech therapist on a regular basis; we have regular appointments with a physio, operational therapist and the pain team specialists. Yes, we are lucky, but none of this happened over night…it's taken nearly five years to gradually get all these specialists in place. We also see a clinical psychologist as the impact of living with daily chronic pain as impacted on Katie in many ways.

For all those parents going through the issues that NF can throw at you my advice would be to stay strong and positive. Don't get me wrong I've had lots of times when I've cried and cried, but, I firmly believe that building up a strong support network of specialists and family/friends helps you…and your child…deal with anything.

By: Davina Smith, (Katie's Mum)

R.I.P My Beloved son David
David's Story:

David arrived into my life three weeks early and as a baby he had the usual childhood ailments but wasn't poorly very often. When he was about four or five he caught a chest infection and it was during an examination the GP commented on his café-au-lait spots. I told the GP they are the same as mine as I have NF Type 1, this is the moment I was told David also had the condition. It came as a huge shock as no one had ever told me it was genetic, but I wasn't overly worried as at this point I didn't really know just how bad NF could be. There were no lumps or bumps on David at all, but we did start to notice he wasn't as forward in certain areas of his schooling and he did have speech problems and was receiving speech therapy.

The problems with his learning started to become apparent and his motor skills were poor. By the time he started his secondary school it became clear that David had dyspraxia and he was dyslexic as well, we had to fight to get him statemented and went to a tribunal, which we won and a statement of educational needs was issued. Came too late to have any real help with his schooling, it was also around this time we discovered he also had mild scoliosis and needed x-rays yearly to check it wasn't getting any worse.

David left school and decided to go to college on a Computer Course which he loved doing and did two years and passed, he decided he would do the third year but within months he became unhappy due to the fact he started to notice he was different from his peers and he left. It was around this time it was discovered I had a MPNST wrapped around my sciatic nerve and needed surgery and radiotherapy. We still didn't know just how bad NF could be as we just thought I was unlucky to be in the minority. David then complained of a lump on his left breast, which was large and we had it checked out; it was a NF lump but there was nothing sinister about it. From this point David stopped being seen for his NF and we started to see if we could get some help in boosting his confidence and trying to improve his living skills, as even though he was 17 he couldn't run a bath, cook a meal or do the usual things most teenagers should be able to do. Everywhere we went we were told the answer "he doesn't meet the criteria" and they had never even met or spoken to him. So David was put on Incapacity Benefit and was told by a panel of doctors that in their estimation they didn't think David would be ready for work by the time he was 25.

In April of last year he complained of backache and was seen by a doctor who said it was muscular due to the position he sat at his computer, but it never really went away and he would need a hot water bottle most days to ease it. It was Sept 26th when he started being sick and this was most unusual as he was rarely sick and had a healthy appetite. Again the doctor was called and a locom came out to see him and diagnosed a stomach bug. From that day David stopped eating properly and his weight started to drop, as he was living with my mother, she took him back to the doctor and this was the first time they actually examined him. The doctor found a lump in his abdomen and said "I see you have an appointment on Friday with your own GP I suggest you keep it and let him examine David". Friday 2nd Nov, David was examined and sent for an ultrasound scan, the results were a mass in his abdomen so he was admitted to hospital and had a CT Scan the following day. All they seemed concerned about was his weight loss and lack of appetite and had him classed as anorexic, which I was furious and upset about.

The general surgeon informed us there was a tumor and his NF was complicating things and David would need to be seen at The Royal Marsden Hospital, so they allowed David to come home, this was 7th Nov. Twelfth Nov David was readmitted to Musgrove Park Hospital where they inserted a feeding tube – luckily a bed became available at Royal Marsden and on 16th Nov he was transferred there; as it was a Friday not much happened over the weekend. He was seen by Prof Thomas who said the tumor was in two parts and part was a cyst that they could drain. There became an issue with David's blood pressure as it was very high and at one point they suspected his tumor was being fed by his adrenal gland so the procedure was cancelled until they could get a consultant anesthetist, and finally on the Thurs it went ahead. I was with him right up until he was put under and as soon as they were bringing him round they rang me and asked me to come back as I had promised David I would be there. I was allowed to stay in recovery with him as well. It was in recovery I noticed at last his blood pressure was normal and I was so relieved, although this was to be short lived as I was told this in fact was bad as it had dropped so rapidly.

The following day, 23rd Nov, was the day my world crashed when Prof Thomas informed me he could not remove the tumor as David's aorta ran through the middle but at this point the results of the biopsy wasn't back. I had to tell my mum the bad news and she immediately made plans to come to London the following day to be with us. Mum arrived to find David having a blood transfusion as his haemoglobin had dropped. On the 26th Nov we were told it was cancer: a sarcoma and a rare one and there was no treatment available, so this was the day we had to tell David he was not going to get better and he had a few tears and he never mentioned it again, just seemed to accept it.

On the 29th Nov David was transferred to St Margaret's Hospice in Somerset, closer to home and I travelled in the ambulance with him and the ward sister as David had a pain relief driver and also needed more pain relief on the trip back. Mum came back via coach. I stayed with David until about 6pm that evening and my older brother came to pick me up and drive to Mum's, I knew at this point he only had days left and not weeks as I had been told a few days earlier. I said goodbye and that I would be back later and he said promise you will come back, so I said "I promise son I will be back I love you" – that was the last time I saw him alive as I didn't go back that evening because I was so tired after spending two weeks virtually 24/7 with him.

I received a phone call at 5.03 on 30th Nov telling me David was very poorly and didn't have long, but by the time we got to the Hospice he had already gone. My darling son was gone and I wasn't there when it happened. We went in and saw him to say goodbye and it was when we sat back in the lounge area I received a text from David that said "having a rough night wish you were here", he had sent that text at 2.07am and I only received it at 6.32am. This was the point I realised just how dangerous NF was and I hated the condition and wished to God I had never had it, as I wouldn't have passed it on. It was only three months later when I felt I needed to know what happened in those final hours that I learned David had in fact passed away two mins after they rang me so there was no way we would ever have made it to be with him.

By: Shirley Rossi Jelley.

My Story Quentin John

This story is about my son Quentin John Laret! Quentin was our surprise baby and our blessing from God since we had miscarried twice before having his older brother, Brendan. They are 17 months apart and when deciding to have children we knew we had a 50/50 chance of having a child with NF since my husband, Matthew also has NF1. When Brendan arrived things looked good and he had tested negative for the gene. When Quentin was born there were signs that I just did not want to believe. By nine months we met with genetics, waiting and watching, and at 19 months symptoms were evident for sure: café au lait marks, hair growth on his face, tumor behind his right ear and on his gum line…he was officially tested and has NF1. That was the beginning of debulkings and treatments. By the time he was two his NF had taken over creating a large right side plexi-form on his head and face that was going to be almost impossible to treat. I made it my mission to educate myself, my husband (since when we were kids education was limited), our families, friends, and community.

We attempted to get involved in a trial study at CHOP, but God had other plans, and we ended up at Cincinnati Children's Hospital. After researching on the Children's Tumor Foundation website we felt he may qualify for another trial study being offered. He did try the medication for three months and his tumor continued to grow…at that point we knew surgery was the only option to ensure any type of quality of life and preserve some level of functionality. Through all of this he has had blood draws, sees fourteen doctors between two hospitals (Nationwide Children's Hospital in Columbus, Ohio) various hospital visits and surgeries…he is like any other kid!!

Fast-forward to 2013, Quentin is six years old...he has had nine surgeries, several complications which led to other treatments and surgeries and he is slated for two more surgeries this year. He is starting kindergarten in the fall. His tumor surrounds his right eye and he has NF1 all behind his eye and he has lost his right nerve on his face since his nerve became the tumor, so he has a crooked smile, scars, tumor on his gum line and growth on the back of his head that has already been removed once off his skull and has small neurofibromas on his spine. The stares are difficult and maintaining some level of normality can be challenging when in the back of your mind there is the unknown. However, we owe it to him and his brother to be as normal as possible and when things are good we rock and roll and when they are not our unbelievable support system kicks in to pull us through.

All of this being said, Quentin has a fighting spirit; contagious laugh, and a crooked smile that melts your heart. Then you realize this child has strength beyond words. He has a relationship with God and believes with unwavering faith. and in my heart I know he is destined for awesome things!! He has touched so many people already... We are forever grateful for our gift, Quentin John Laret.

By: Kimberly Laret

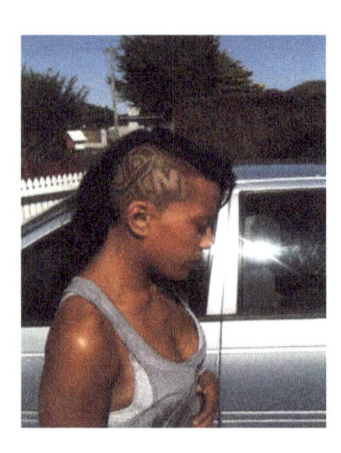

My Story By: Seniar

It's crazy how far back I remember certain events that took place in my life as a kid, especially how some of them made me feel.

I remember one particular day at school when I was 8 years old, my friend and I were doing handstands when my top went up showing my tummy, another girl yelled out at me "Ew, you got those ugly brown spots all over your tummy" (café-au-laitspots), I never did handstands again. I felt ashamed, sad, and hated my ugly body.

That night I asked my mum if my "ugly brown spots" will ever go away and she said "yes, when you get older". I'm older now, and still got them. I wish my mum knew that I really did believe they'd disappear, but guess Mum was as clueless as me not knowing what they were; even our family doctor never pointed them out every time we visited him.

When I was nine years old it was discovered I was blind in my left eye and being that young I never understood why, doctors couldn't even explain.

Fast-forward 18 years later when I was living in Brisbane Australia, I took the day off work due to having a nasty migraine. Whilst at the doctors getting a checkup I thought I'd ask him about the bump in my palm, he couldn't explain what it was, nor the bump on my foot, so he cut them out and had samples sent away. I still remember my doctor's reaction and response to when the results came back. "Oh no" he said. "What is it?" I responded. "I hate when there's nothing I can do!" he said. I was scared, worried. "Basically, it hasn't hit the tip of the iceburg" was his exact words. I left the clinic that day with documents he had printed off for me from Google to learn about it all on my own. I was diagnosed with Neurofibromatosis Type 1, and only then did things from my past start to make sense: my "ugly brown spots", the loss of vision in my left eye, my bumps, why I struggled in school.

It's taken me a long time to accept my condition and I often struggle at times, especially when I didn't know anyone else who had NF too. Since then, I've participated in Sydney's first ever Cupids Undie Run, a fundraising event where all funds raised go to The Children's Tumor Foundation and help find a cure for children living with NF. I've made friends with people just like me from all over the world, and it's nice to have people who understand exactly what you're going through.

I try to go about my life living as if I don't have NF, but it's hard to forget about it when you have to look at your body every day and see the spots, and tumors, but I'm learning that I can either wake up and worry for the rest of my life about the body God has given me, or I can get over it and enjoy my life. After all, I'm only "renting" this body while I'm here on Earth, I'm guessing once my number is up and I leave this world, my body remains in the ground anyway.

By: Seniar Tufuga.

My Story By: Michelle

My name is Michelle and I am 36yrs old and live with mum in Norwich. My sister, her partner and two young children also live in Norwich, as does my dad. I am the only person in my family to have NF.

I was diagnosed with NF1 when I was five years old and had several trips to Great Ormond Street Hospital when I was young. I now see the doctor at the Norfolk and Norwich University Hospital.

I have several lumps over my body and had two large ones removed from my left arm. These were from armpit to elbow, this took two operations and then elbow to wrist. I also had a metatarsal bone removed from my right foot. This can cause pain and also difficulty fitting shoes. Internally, as far as I know I have three lumps – one on optic nerve, a large one near my adrenal gland and one on my spine. The only one to cause me any trouble is the spinal one as this causes me to have shooting sensations in my left hand fingers.

When I was young I had speech therapy and physiotherapy.

When I was at school I had poor concentration and fine motor (handwriting) problems. For most of my school life I had help from a welfare assistant. I stayed on into the 6th form to do a G.N.V.Q course, following my G.C.S.Es. This led me to do an N.V.Q course at a college in Norwich. During the course at college, I had a placement at the Norfolk and Norwich University Hospital and through this I learned that they had a Clerical and Admin Bank. This is temporary employment when needed. After my course finished I worked through the Clerical Bank for a short while and this led me into my current job. At the beginning I worked fulltime but after a while was assessed under Occupational Health and now work three days a week. Most of my work involves computer skills.

In my personal life I enjoy socialising with friends, going to pubs, cinema or in the city shopping. Mum and I have a Labrador dog and take him for walks, although he is getting too old and arthritic to walk as far as we used to. Sometimes, Mum and I go for longer walks of six to eight miles. It's nice to go on rambles where cars cannot go. Mum and I also go swimming at a local pool. Sometimes we take my three-year-old niece swimming. Every Thursday Mum and I look after my niece while my sister is at work. She's on maternity leave at the moment but when she returns to work, Mum and I will then have the brother of my niece to look after as well. Sometimes we take her to a local zoo or park, but when the weather is not nice we look after her at ours and she loves paint and glitter – what a mess.

Hopefully, Mum and I hope to move in the next few months. Still in Norwich, but we want to buy a smaller place, because of this we are not having a holiday, but in the past years we have enjoyed several holidays. Last year we toured the National Parks in America and saw some really beautiful places.

As you can see I don't let NF hold me back. I work, love looking after my niece and nephew and socialising. Last year Mum and I went to a NF meet in Peterborough and met some wonderful people, who I still keep in contact with. Through the NF website I met a lovely girl who has NF and lives I Norwich. We socialise together every fortnight.

Hopefully my health stays as it is, so I can continue with my lifestyle.

By: Michelle Nobes

My Story By: Bobbie

I am not really sure where to start my story. I guess the beginning is a good place to start.

I knew from my first day in kindergarden that I was not like the other children: a little slower to catch on to new lessons and not as mature.

Our family doctors never found any health concerns for myself in the many years that I went to our family clinic in Nebraska City, Nebraska. In 1970 I had two so-called "fatty tumors" removed that I found out these growths were actually neurofibromas. It would take another two years before the connection between these growths and a disorder called neurofibromatosis was made. The doctors at the Mayo Clinic in Rochester, Minnesota carefully explained to me and my parents the facts about this disorder. No one in the whole family history had this disorder and even heard of it. Neurofibromatosis was a very foreign word to everyone. The doctors at the time told me that I would probably never meet another person with this disorder in my life.

They advised me that it would be wise not to have any children because of the many complications of this disorder.

My overall health was pretty good. The only complications for me were the neurofibromas that could pop up on my body. Most would appear on my torso and could easily be hidden by clothing. Something I could easily deal with. I knew that this disorder was progressive and was not sure what my future held for me.

I did find the man of my dreams and got married in 1973. Against the advice of the doctor at the Mayo Clinic I did get pregnant and had a beautiful baby girl in September of 1974. We named her Christina Marie. Her middle name was after my grandmother Milton who I dearly loved. Right after her birth I had asked the doctors if she showed any signs of having the same disorder as myself. The doctors assured me that there were no cafe-au-lait marks or any signs of her having neurofibromatosis. At that time I thought signs showed up immediately at birth. I did not know that usually it takes a few months for the first signs to appear.

Every day at bathtime I would carefully check Christina for any brown spots or small growths. When she was about three months old the first large cafe-au-lait mark appeared on her leg. It was about two inches long and half an inch wide. Then after that three or four appeared in a short time. I was heartbroken that I had passed this disorder on to my daughter. I knew that inspite of having the same disorder as myself that my daughter could have a wonderful life and I would do everything I could to make her life as wonderful as possible.

While growing up Christina had many of the same problems as myself. She had a hard time in school and was always behind her peers. I saw myself in my daughter's childhood. History just repeated itself.

My hopes for Christina were that she would grow up and find a rewarding career and remain single and be happy with her life. Much like my own parents I had hoped she would not chose to have children. But, if she did I knew she would have my full support. With Christina and myself both having NF I did not want to see a third generation suffer with the any effects of having NF.

When she did decide to have one child I was worried and just hoped that her baby would escape the same genetics as the two of us shared. John Corey was born in 1999. Like his mother he showed no signs of NF at birth. Then those dreaded café-au-laitspots appeared. Now we were three generations of NF. John Corey also had a mild case of autism with his NF. Some children with NF also have cases of autism.

I never thought I had to worry about my own daughter. I found out on the night of April 21, 2012 that she had been taken to the hospital with internal bleeding. The doctors told us they had stopped the bleeding but were not sure she would survive. There were few documented cases of NF were someone can have blood vessels that can burst and the person will bleed into their lungs. She had what doctors call a thoracic aortic aneurysm and lost two thirds of her blood. The doctors told me this would have never happened except for the fact she had NF. There were few documented cases of this happening to other NF patients. In all my research I had never heard of this I felt guilty for passing the NF gene on to my only child.

With the skill and care of two wonderful doctors Dr. Rao Gutta and Dr. John Batter from Omaha, Nebraska my daughter did make it through this crisis and her two children had their mother back. It took over a year for Christina to learn how to manage the pain. With faith and a lot of help from her husband Christina has recovered and is back to being a wonderful mother to her two children John Corey and Sofie. She has a positive attitude towards life and is a wonderful daughter, mother, and friend to many.

Dealing with NF is very difficult and everyone has his or her own journey in life dealing with it. For me the cosmetic effects are the hardest. We live in a society where so much emphasis is placed on appearance and the way we look. I wish I could go back and have the fibroma free skin I had at 18. I know that will not happen. I just have to find a way to be at peace with this disorder. Perhaps an impossible task for myself.

By: Bobbie Colgan

My Story By: Nikole

Don't Judge a Body by its Cover: Nikole Davis, Oregon

When I was around ten or 11 years old, I was having extreme pains in my lower back, shooting pains in fact and that's when my dad finally decided to seek medical attention. That is when I had my first minor surgery followed by another as they grew back and were deeper. When the results came back it was scary as we did not have internet let alone much knowledge of this disease. I was just told it was "Elephant Man" disease and eventually I would be as deformed as he was. At ten years old, that was insanely uncomforting.

Years went by and I moved to Portland and was having an episode where I could not even walk. The doctor said I was obese and this was all in my head, and there is no chance that I have NF and he was sure of it. When I asked why, he said, "YOU DON'T LOOK

LIKE YOU HAVE IT and if you lost a few pounds you would be in less pain!" He said it was just muscle strain. Here are some drugs.

Within the next couple days, my back was so black and blue I couldn't even eat, I went to the ER and again was told that this is in my head and I don't have it as I don't look like someone with NF. They tested me for other things but refused to make me comfortable as they thought I was just another pill seeker. Then proceeded to accuse my boyfriend of beating me. Then said it was a muscle strain. I thought, what the hell is this muscle strain BS? My lower back is almost black!

Years later, I was having so much right shoulder pain, after several MRI's nothing was working to help pain levels; I was told I had mass in my shoulder. I went to a specialist that knows about my disease, and I went to a few surgeons who all said that they could not operate on my shoulder as it would paralyze me and that they strongly suggest that I learn how to use my left hand as it will most likely become my dominate hand. They said that there is a lot of damage there and eventually even if they did not operate, I would end up paralyzed on the right side. One of them said that they can't operate because they would not be able to cut the tumors out without hitting a nerve and the tumors are all imbedded in the brachial plexus. They just will continue to grow and multiply if you can't get all of it. I have actually talked to eight or nine surgeons that have all said no to surgery and there's nothing they can do except ask my preference of pain pills. Just way too dangerous!

A couple years later my right shoulder was so flared up that I could not even move. I was given Xanax, Dilaudid, Amitriptyline, Percocet, Morphine timed release, and Morphine to be taken every couple hours. Try not to mix any of the above. The doctor told me that if it didn't help within the next day that I was going to be admitted and he would document this. Well, a couple days later I found myself sitting in the ER waiting room for five hours, they said they did not see in my chart where the doctor said to admit me.

When laying in the ER room almost comatose from so much Dilaudid going through my veins, they finally agreed to admit me because again, Dilaudid wasn't working, just making me very tired.

I asked for Phenergan to stop the nausea and was told no. Sadly, I got sick. This nurse came in to take the blood pressure cuff off (my right arm, where all the pain is) and instead of doing it carefully she threw my arm up and ripped it off so fast I about died as she said, "Got to Do It Quickly!" I was in tears and, well, threw up again as I was in so much pain. These people were treating me as if I was a drug seeker.

The following October the tumors in my left breast were unbearable and sometimes these pains would stop me in my tracks. I went to the doctor again, and yet again was passed off to another doctor. I thought for sure I found THE one to help me as he was determined to stop the pain from continuing. He ordered an ultrasound and a mammogram and said if that didn't show anything he would go in and do an exploratory surgery as he was pretty sure that there is a tiny tumor there that may have not been detected. I waited a while to get a mammogram appointment and was told by the scheduler that I was too young for these tests because I was too young to get cancer. I had to ask them if they have been to Dornbecher lately and how am I too young to get cancer. They said they are sorry but they have to wait to get radiologist approval as sometimes doctors just have tests done just to have them done. I asked them why it's up to the radiologist, as they are not my doctor and should not have the final say. I ended up calling the head of radiology and pitched a fit. I told them they have one of two choices, either get my mammogram scheduled or to talk to my attorney. They said that there was no need for getting an attorney involved. I literally laughed and said what's it going to be? The woman I was speaking to looked at my file and said oh my, it was missed. I said to her what was that? She said the doctor marked this urgent. You are messing with something that could be potentially serious? I said well then I guess you need to schedule it NOW!! Thankfully nothing was on the mammogram or ultrasound but unfortunately the doctor who was going to help me died suddenly of a heart attack. I was passed off to another doctor who was on his cell phone talking about sports and such and wasting my time. He told me there is nothing there, he won't do surgery and I need to see a lung specialist. I asked why is one doctor willing to go in and cut the nerve to prevent all this pain and you just want to pass me off? He said that it is just not the best thing to do for you at this time. Still on his phone I might add. I said choice words as I walked out.

Since all of this and more, I have finally found a doctor who has listened and suggested low dose Lyrica which is not necessarily something I want to take, but has helped me tremendously. I recommend it for nerve pain! This doctor has said to me that NF pain is REAL! Finally someone in the medical field who does not judge a body by its cover!

By: Nikole Davis

My Story By: Veronica

I was born in July of 1979 and raised on a farm with my parents and older brother and sister and younger brother. I lost my mother to breast cancer on St. Patrick's Day, 1998; after a year and a half my dad married a widow with five children (four boys and a girl), then along came my little brother in March of 2002.

Growing up with Neurofibromatosis and scoliosis, I was slower when it came to field days and school subjects like math and science. However, with teacher's aides, lots of hard work, and determination, I graduated high school with my friends and went on to college by correspondence studying Early Childhood Education.

In the summer of 1994, I got a job babysitting for the family down the road; as the years went by, and I watched the family grow from two little girls to five children, I came to realize children never judge you by what you look like or what you wear but by characteristics like kindness, humour, and creativity. I love those children as if they were my own, spoiling them at Christmas, birthdays, and Easter, and whenever I had the chance. They will always have a special place in my heart. If only the people you meet on the street and in the mall were like children instead of staring at you because you have something on your skin.

From August 2002 through April 2010, after seven and half years of dedication and hard work, I left the retirement home to open a new door. When I started working at the retirement home I was working in dietary and laundry. Within a year, I became the fulltime laundry aide working nights while getting settled in the job and looking for my own apartment in town closer to my work place. With the help of my aunt, I got on the list for subsidized housing; once settled in my apartment, I adopted my kitten which came with the name Mocha; a sweet siamese who I trained to walk on a harness and leash, play fetch, and is a wonderful companion.

One night while working with the nurse, we were going to the smoke room as she was a smoker, linked arm and arm, I by accident hit the bumps and lumps on my arms and I was like "ouch my woogies" and so from that day forward when small children ask what are the bumps on my skin I tell them "woogies".

Through working at the retirement home I worked the night shift with a co-worker name Collette. Over the years we became the best of friends. She and her children have become a part of my life, remembering them at Christmas and birthdays. Her children have always looked past my physical appearance and love me unconditionally.

In November of 2010 I got a job at a thrift store where I sort the clothes that fill the store. Each day is full of surprises as you never know what you will sort that day; whether it be a funny shirt or name brand pair of jeans, or a cute dress. In April of 2011 an opportunity came available to transfer to another city. I applied and was very excited that I got the transfer and in July I packed up Mocha, and the apartment said good-bye to my co-workers and friends and moved closer to my cousins.

Living with Neurofibromatosis has had it challenges through the years with pain in my back and hips. To date as I write my story in July of 2013 I've never had any major surgery for my back or the woogies.

However In May of 2011 I had two woogies removed from my right hand otherwise I've manage to live with them even the itchy ones.

In conclusion, that's the story of my life in short form, I'm grateful that I have such a wonderful family, including my cousins, aunts, and uncles for being so loving and caring. I'm blessed to have such a wonderful group of friends to work with at the thrift store; and specially my best friend Collette who told me about NF groups on Facebook and for always being so loving and caring. And even though NF is painful and hard to live with I can still say Thank you, Lord, for giving me NF as perhaps I've touched some peoples lives in the past and hopefully will continue to do so in the future. I believe God only gives each of us the weight of a cross that He knows we can bear. As I've heard from some of my NF family near and far on Facebook "I HAVE NEUROFIBROMATOSIS BUT IT DOESN'T HAVE ME".

By: Veronica Stevers

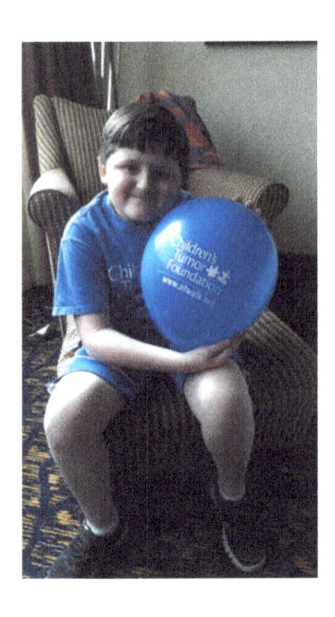

Seth Luellen's NF Story.

My son Seth Luellen has NF 1. He was diagnosed a little over two years ago which threw me through a loop again after already knowing and dealing with his chromosome duplication that had caused so many disorders and seven food allergies, and yes severe at that. But the summer before his 3rd grade year his allergist that was just doing a routine exam and checkup on his skin disorders asked me when he started getting all the freckles and kind of big birth marks. I said well he just started getting them out of nowhere and I thought it was just another odd thing, no biggie, but he said he needed to be further tested as he thought he was in the neurofibromatosis category which I just assumed was another skin disorder that they always said he might get, I had no clue what it really was and I didn't even look it up when I got home, I was so use to him developing new skin disorders and other allergies I just went with the flow.

So I called the derma doc and set up an appointment with her, she did confirm it and next was back to the genetic team which we already had due to other genetic problems. Once there at that appointment in Lousiville Kentucky, the team of doctors looked at the paperwork and results from the allergist and his derma doc and started doing their testing asap but they were worried and was ordering MRIs and scans and NF eye doctors and more – I was just wondering what the fuss was about " I said it's just another skin disorder right?" Then I got my reality check as they were counting all the café-au-lait spots and freckles in the armpits and said maybe that's why his head is so big; we had a road and a half ahead of us again.

We have a lot more doctors and specialist now. Seth has a mass behind his left eye and two different eye doctors we have to go to every six months to make sure he doesn't need chemo to shrink it; one is in Kentucky and one in Ohio which is an ocular oncologist. It's scary with NF. He also has the chronic pain from NF that started up, and takes two more meds for that; he's developed autism, a tic syndrome, a cyst in his brain, swelling in one section of his brain; has speech disorders, sleep apena, an aortic heart valve disease, restless leg syndrome, tons of developmental delays and much more. We have a total of 36 active doctors and therapists we see and over 30 meds to this day to keep him going… we all pray for a cure for NF.

By: Robin Black

My Story by Jennifer Renee'

My name is Jennifer Renee' Berube, I am 51 years old and have NF. I am the fourth daughter of Andrew Berube and Jean Berube.

When I was born on December 4th 1962 I had many health issues. One issue was a large lump on my head and they were concerned that as I got older and started moving around I would bump it and break it open and could bleed to death so we had it removed.

As I got older my father and grandfather noticed I was not developing like I should have been. My eyes were very crossed and I had a lazy eye. I ended up having many surgeries to correct this, which caused me to have a tracheotomy at the age of two.

My fine and large motor skills were not were they should be. I spent a lot of time in the hospital in my young life. My parents were divorcing and my birth mother left when I was less than a year old. My grandfather was there to take care of my sisters and me when my father was at work. My father remarried when I was five, and his new wife could see a lot of potential in me she could not believe that the doctors had labeled me (retarded). She pushed me to reach for my goals and to do anything I wanted to do and that I was not retarded.

School was difficult academically and getting along with my peers was hard. The kids were brutal, I was bullied all through school. By both teachers and students. When I hit puberty it got worse. Not only did I struggle academically but I still had the coordination problems. That is when I started getting the Neuromas on my arms legs and chest area, which was difficult to dress down for me because they were very visible. I would dress in the bathroom stall so no one would see me or the bumps.

As I have gotten older things have not gotten any easier. My bumps have gotten bigger and I have gotten a lot more bumps, which has required surgery; I don't know how many times because I have lost count. In the last two years I have been diagnosed with Scoliosis Osteoporosis all due to early menopause due to the NF. I am getting more and more of the tumors on my face, neck, feet, chest, legs and back.

In 2012 they took off over 500 just on my back alone. The arthritis in my hips and spine make it difficult to walk and stand at times. This is also a result of the NF. The stares, looks and comments from supposedly mature adults is the hardest thing about this disorder for me. I had a job working in a laundry for 20 years. I was not treated nicely by some of my co-workers there. They thought they could catch what I had even though they had worked with me for over 15 years. I did everything I could to teach them that what I had was a birth defect and they could not get it. Their little remarks would upset me and I tried to ignore them but in the end I was not able to. With not being able to ignore their hurtful remarks and I would end up getting in trouble so I finally took a job in a different department and my new co-workers treat me with a lot more respect.

The hardest thing about having NF is the disfigurement and having to look at yourself in the mirror. When all you can see is the bumps. I do not see myself as a beautiful person physically. All I can see is the bumps. I know physically appearance does not make the person and it's what's inside that really counts. How you treat others is more important. I feel that I treat people with a lot of respect and in turn I can make a lot of friendships that last a lifetime. I have one very close friend who has stuck with me forever, we have been friends since we were toddlers. I have many friends that I have met over the years. I have the best family that anybody can have. My parents believed in me and encourage me to do anything I wanted, now that they are gone I have my sisters to turn to and they have been there for me through thick and thin I am very lucky to have the sisters that I do. I love them very much I don't know what I would have done without them.

I knew I could not have children in fear of passing this disorder on to them, so I decided that I would adopt. I became a foster parent and had a young lady come live with me at the age of eight. She is now 21 and doing great. I don't like the fact that she has had to take a lot of bullying from her own peers because of the way I look, that has bothered me the most. She would get bullied because she would defend me when rude comments were made by her classmates, she has also lost friends because the parents didn't want their child around her because of the way I looked. All in all I have a daughter that really loves me. Thank-you for taking the time to read our stories and learning something about NF, and how it affects all of us!

By: Jennifer Renee' Berube

My Story: Jaimee Grace.

My name is Jaimee Grace Bouwer. I'm 11 years old. To be honest I don't like wearing a brace because it is uncomfortable, especially when it is hot. Lots of things upset me because I have scholiosis. Like I don't have a lot of friends, and I really don't fit it. I have struggled to learn at school and I don't feel pretty. My brace upsets me, and that's why sometimes I shout at people, but where other people hurt them they forgive them but not me. But I'm glad because I can get really nice grown up clothes not children's clothes.

Sometimes I'm not the happiest girl in the world. My parents help me every step of the way. They love me for who I am.

By: Jaimee Grace Bouwer

Michelle: Jaimee's Mom's Story

Jaimee was diagnosed with NF on the 23 August 2003 at the age of 1yr 10 months by her paediatrician. A geneticist confirmed it was a 'spontaneous mutation' two months later. Besides the café au lait and freckling, life continued as normal. At this stage her skin condition was undiagnosed and we were sent from one dermatologist to the next, each with their own diagnosis and method of treatment. Unknown to us this would escalate and cause my daughter unbearable suffering. She started Pre-Primary at Collegiate Junior, an all-girls' school at the age of four. The year before formal school began her class teacher called us in to have a chat. We were told she was not coping with new work, that she was tearful and emotionally immature and it was her recommendation that she be kept back another year. This request was turned down by the Headmistress. We started Occupational Therapy to help Jaimee with her gross motor abilities, a Psychologist to help her with social and emotional readiness and a Speech Therapist to assist with her pronunciation and auditory processing.

One evening my husband was helping her to dry off after a bath when he noticed that her hips were not in alignment. This was another new development on her 'bumpy' road. We took her to an orthopaedic surgeon and scoliosis was confirmed. We were told to 'wait and see' as the curvature was only 8* and nothing could be done at this stage.

In the meantime her skin condition worsened and she would scratch herself until she bled. She was hospitalized in the Greenacres Netcare Private Hospital for two days and covered from neck to ankles in bandages; called the wet-wrap bandage method. This was done 3x daily with tears rolling down her face.

Second-degree infection set in and we were sent down to the Red Cross Hospital in Cape Town for a biopsy. This all resulted in a staph infection which resisted antibiotics and her own immune system began attacking her. Not one doctor told me that this was related to NF. I found that "Pruritis" (itchy skin) is a rare spin off from NF during my research from the internet. I had diagnosed her condition myself. Whilst this was going on, Jaimee was being extremely bullied at school. None of the girls would play with her at break-time and if she sat down next to anyone they would move away. During a consult I asked a certain dermatologist if Jaimee was allowed to swim and he told me in front of her "I am sure the other mothers would not like their children to swim in the same water as her!' I was dumb-founded by his lack of tact. By then her self-esteem was at an all time low with the girl's comments and staring. We bought her a one-piece uni-leotard to swim in. I would collect Jaimee from school with tears running down her face. She was sitting by herself and nobody wanted to play with her. She started seeing the school counsellor. I eventually made an appointment with a Psychiatrist who advised "melatonin" to assist her in sleeping and placed Jaimee on chronic medication for anxiety. It has now been three years and I don't see any sign of her being able to stop the medication.

In the interim her spine had continued to worsen and we were given an ultimatum from a Professor Robert Dunn at a spinal clinic in Cape Town. Either wait and perform a "spinal fusion' once she reached 40* or place her in a body brace to prevent the curvature from progressing. It wasn't an easy decision to make but we felt we had to try to avoid surgery. A Plaster of Paris mould was made and her first brace was fitted on the 5 September 2011. She was given a two-week programme to build up to the recommended hours. Jaimee now wears a Boston Brace 23 hours a day. How do you explain to your precious daughter that what you are doing is for her best interest? You question whether you are doing the right thing. So many tears have been shed by myself and Jaimee. Hearts shattered, glued back together and then broken again. The meltdowns. The insecurity. The self-hatred, and her questions towards her faith. Her unhappiness increased. My heart stopped when she told me 'that she wishes she could throw herself in front of a car and die'…she was ten years old. A list was given to her by a 'so-called' friend listing what others thought of her. None of it was pleasant and she was devastated. Once again my husband and I met with the Headmistress, Class Teacher and School Guidance teacher to discuss that my daughter was still being victimised (now for two years). We were assured the matter would be dealt with.

At this stage NF was raising its ugly head and she was beginning to struggle with her schoolwork. She doesn't know how to socially interact with her peers and to this day has not got one best friend. Birthday party invites and sleepovers are not extended to her. Her poor motor-skills makes playing sport hard and basic skills others take for granted take extra time and concentration, eg swimming and bicycle riding. Dermal fibromas were increasing and the girls at school were beginning to ask why she had so many 'bumps'. I became concerned when online groups advised that all NF and scoliosis children should have MRIs done. Seeing that Jaimee does not have a NF team working with her (due to reason that RSA does not have any specialised NF doctors or clinics available) I persuaded her geneticist to send a request for a MRI to be done. This was performed last year with no sedation given.

Two separate scans were done: one of the brain and thoracic and lumbar spine, and the second MRI of her chest to see if her plexiform tumour could be removed. It had become painful to the touch and was increasing in size. The news brought mixed feelings. There were no tumours alongside her spinal cord. The plexiform had not entwined itself along any major blood vessels and was not deep. They had however, found three lesions in her brain which according to a neurosurgeon are consistent with NF and just need to be monitored unless speech or movement problems are noted. Not reassuring at all!

Then on 30 September 2012 our world was once again shaken. Jaimee had her first seizure and stopped breathing. She was rushed to hospital. An EEG test was performed but came back negative. The seizures continued and she was diagnosed with Epilepsy and placed on medication. NF had once again shown us just how unpredictable it was. This has changed our family dynamic. We are constantly aware and listening for where she is. Her older siblings have been shown what to do when she has a Grand-Mal or Absence Seizure. She is not allowed to bathe on her own, swim on her own or even ride her bicycle alone. I have to attend all school outings with her, watch her during her PT swim class during school and attend her swimming classes after school. If I don't do this, the school will not allow her to partake at all. Each and every time Jaimee has had a seizure, eg in the swimming pool, alone in the study, riding her bicycle in the street, in the school classroom our Lord Jesus has been there to protect her and keep her safe.

Jaimee was admitted again to the Greenacres Hospital on the 25 October 2012 to remove NF tumours. Three subcutaneous tumours were removed from base of her neck, lower spine and torso. One plexiform was removed from her chest. This was the first time we have had to have tumours removed. As she is approaching puberty we have noticed more and more fibromas appearing.

But who is Jaimee Grace Bouwer? She is fun loving, loyal, sympathetic to those in need and friendly. She has inner and outer beauty with a faith in Christ to help her overcome all of life's ups and downs. She has an infectious laugh and joyful spirit. She loves to dance, cook, read and play games. She enjoys hockey and swimming. She belongs to Scripture Union and the Computer Club at school. She loves all animals and abhors cruelty. She loves watching Cartoon Network, musicals and Zac Efron. Jaimee has NF but it will never have her. We leave our precious princess in the Lord's hands. He is our strength and her strength. I stand amazed and inspired with Jaimee. We call her our Scoli-Warrior but in actual fact she is a Princess of the Most High God.

One step one day at a time…

By: Michelle Bouwer

My Story By Mike.

My name is Mike Turk, I was born in June 1967 with NF. My father had it, as did his mother, who sadly I never recall meeting ever when I was growing up. One thing I remember being told was she was barred from my dad's eldest brother's wedding. The reason being was her NF; it was severe especially on her face, and I think remarks were made in respect of wedding photos being ruined, which I thought was a nasty and cruel thing to say. So my own NF experience didn't really show until I was about nine, when the tumours, (Fibromas) started to appear.

My experiences were enduring stares and people elbowing there friends and nodding in my direction when I went the baths, or the beach. So at that age I was becoming self- conscious, and this resulted in my swimming, and sunbathing days to a end at the age of ten. When I started high school things worsened, especially when it came to Games, or P.E. I would pull a sickie, or intentionally forget my kit, but sometimes it was unavoidable and I had to take part, so I would ensure I was last out to the Games field to avoid people seeing my NF, which was becoming more evident.

When taking part if the ball ever hit me on the back the pain was excruciating even today a friendly pat on the back hurts. At the end of the games lesson, I would not shower until I got home and games being the last lesson on a Thursday, it was easier to wait till I got home.

During my teens when the few friends I had started seeing girls, I had less success once they found out I had NF, they decided they like me more as a friend which was a poor excuse just because I was different, so I was reluctant to try anymore. By the time I was 18, I moved out into my own flat during the eighties were I tried to end my life but a friend saved me, his name was Chris Pinch, and thanks to him I am here today. NF was eating me up after another relationship I struck up ended, I thought I was never going to meet someone who would except me NF an all, there wasn't a lot of information available then that I was aware of back then. When it came to getting interviews for possible employment I had to inform them of my NF and was asked questions about whether they leaked, or became pussy, which I found insulting, and upsetting. As a result I found myself dressing for winter all year round whatever the weather and avoiding crowds. It wasn't till my 30s that I met my current partner Angela (wife) wedded for the last two years, but been together for 12 years now who I knew when I was a teenager, but we never seen one another again once I had left home.

Today Angela tries to reassure me and to ignore the looks and stares I still endure today, my life has changed so much that I have started going the baths again albeit I do wear a short wet suit when swimming. She truly does except me NF and all, so much so we have two daughters, Emma nine, and Amy seven. Unfortunately both my daughters have been diagnosed with NF and fibromas are now starting to show both were diagnosed from birth really from the café au lait patches, which is one of the ways of knowing for sure if someone has NF, and to top that off both have been diagnosed with several other conditions ADHD, ASD, DYSPRAXIA and other communication related conditions.

Over the last several years since birth it's been a struggle seeing all kinds of health professionals, and getting the right help and medicines to treat the above. Emma has also been diagnosed with Scoliosis which was picked up on a scan for an unrelated condition so another scan was done to confirm it was Scoliosis and we are waiting to find out to what extent. Both our girls are on medication for the above Emma is taking Strattera, Melatonin, Fluoxetine, Pizotifen, and mebeverine. Amy is also on Melatonin, and Equasym over the last several years we have seen specialist including Christine Stieger, Rosemary Abbott and many more to whom me and Angela, thank very much for their help.

In today's society people are more ruthless than when I was young, especially the younger generation when it comes to fitting in. I still doubt myself even with my wife supporting me but I need to be strong for her and especially my daughters, I don't want them suffering like I did for all them years.

By: Mike Turk

My mom's (Beverley) story:

Hayley Peta Marrs delivered by me, Beverley, and perfect in every way.

To the delight and fascination of all the nurses in the maternity ward of Woodside Hospital, Fremantle, Western Australia; this baby girl was born with long hair dark and when they held her into the sunlight they discovered blonde tips on her fine, soft, delicate hair ends.

Gentle and so soft to caress was this little baby and in the first weeks I thought the crying was the sign of an unsettled baby in a house with five older siblings.

At six weeks while bathing my baby I discovered birthmarks but why so many of them?

I remember all this as if it was yesterday. My doctor really had no answer; he thought they were also birthmarks.

Months went by and this delicate little girl didn't eat very well, had a very bad flu at around six months and although you know your baby isn't developing and reaching the milestones you somehow love them too much to see.

I remember one lunchtime break watching the Mike Walsh show on TV. There was a lady talking about a genetic disorder called NF. I listened and a cold chill went right through me; I knew my innocent little baby had this NF, I cried.

Living with Neurofibromatosis By: Hayley:

"NF is much different as the next like a fingerprint".

My name is Hayley and I have Neurofibromatosis type one and this is my story.

NF1 has been a challenge for me and even today but I still thrive every day.

Everyone's life is different; we walk different paths and experience different things. The more experience we gain the stronger we get, Many things were different for me but I never have let anything stand in my way and my mom and family have done everything for me to lead a normal happy life. Ways to develop my abilities and to make new friends.

I have a big family of four brothers and two sisters, none of them have NF besides me and my nanna's brother Ron. From the age of eight you could say that I was a challenge, not really like a normal eight year old with the same likes and dislikes and a bit cheeky, like what is normal. Anyway my school report said I was "easily distracted" and I "tried".

I got my eyes tested and had a general checkup with the neurologist doctor at Perth's Children's Hospital, I also had MRI scans.

Once I hit my teen years tumors started to become more viable, this started me feeling unsure I don't think I was aware I had NF I was basically misunderstood and teased we moved around a lot as a child I went to many different schools, and at each school I was called all sort of horrid names, "retard". As high school went on my NF started to show more on my body "lumps" on my skin showed more and people in school properly wondered what was wrong with me I had one girl ask if I had "rabies" or "moles" and even a teacher once ask "do you have chicken poxs?" "People are scared of what they don't understand" and special education was always my safety net there were other high school kids from mainstream who just saw the disability before the person.

My friend Faye made up our own family where we created a famous father and mother that we were adopted by, "making up games was part of who I was", she quoted to me. I feel that I always need to keep an eye on how NF is taking over me, sometimes I just feel the pain is unbearable.

So today I can say that even though I have NF the downside is all those MRIs but I have to say I feel so upset and sad and alone when I see people stare at me and some may judge me before they get to know me; I find it hard to make friends.

I joined a group and become a spokesperson for people with disabilities we also did camps with this group and held and ran meetings. I cannot explain how hard it is to talk about having NF, but once I trust a person I tell them and explain.

I am really good at photography and working with children I did complete my Level 3. I got a job in childcare, after I left that job I got a temp nanny job with a family and my brother with my nephew.

When I started meeting people on Facebook with NF I never thought I would meet such amazing talented people. I have friends I speak to almost daily and I could never imagine my life without them it has made my life as a growing person easy. I hope to meet a few in person someday as I have met some already and some of them I've stayed in contact, with others we have moved on. I feel there needs to be a lot more understanding and people need to read and learn about NF. Wherever my NF life takes me I always remember someone has told me "I have NF but it dose not have me".

By: Haley Marrs

My Story By: Rebecca

So I will tell you a little about my experience with NF. First of all, I have NF1, which is the milder form so I guess I'm kind of lucky. I was diagnosed at the age of four. It was mostly due to my parents noticing all my café-au-lait spots and freckles, and my complaining of my chin and mouth hurting. They discovered that I had a plexiform neurofibroma growing under the floor of my mouth, and it was beginning to poke through into my mouth. They had me go for a CAT scan and an MRI at Geisinger Medical Center in Danville, Pennsylvania. After about a year and a half when I had just turned six they decided they should remove it, but that they couldn't get the part poking through the floor of my mouth, so that part's still there, but it doesn't really bother me. I remember being in the hospital for like three days and that I told them I didn't want pain medicine because I have a high tolerance for pain, even then. Also I missed the first day of 1st grade since it took place in August. (I was so upset).

For a long time I didn't have any other problems, but lately, like the past two years I've been having problems again. I've had too many MRIs to count, and in the past year I had to get two more surgeries on my chest and back. Once in August, and again in December, although these took place at CHOP (children's hospital of Philadelphia). I still have plenty more lumps, but most are under my skin so you can't see them, or even know that they are there.

In regards to the rather large one in my neck I just had a three-hour long MRI done, but they had to knock me out because not many people can stay perfectly still for three hours straight. Could you? But I don't complain much; compared to some people with the disorder I don't have a very severe case. I do have a few other symptoms; I get migraines, which cause insomnia occasionally, and I get some pain/itching at the tumors above my skin. Other than that it's not so bad to deal with.

By: Rebecca Salen

My Story by: Mandy

Hello everyone my name is Mandy, I was born with NF1 and I am now 57 years old.

As I child very little was known about this condition, all of my school life I suffered from bulling. I have a large brown mark everyone used to say I had a tea stain on my leg and my bumps were caused because I didn't wash. It was a horrible time for me I was called thick and stupid by teachers saying she has the ability but won't use it so my parents labelled me lazy and constantly punished me. I now know now it's because I have a learning disability.

All of my life I have been stared at, people have moved tables to get away from me, it hurts, I sometimes respond by saying 2would you like a photo, its rude to stare", other times I leave in tears. A few weeks ago I was having a coffee in a shop and a gentleman was staring at me he said to his wife "look at her you wouldn't think she would go out looking like that", his wife turned and stared and tutted, this time I said something, I was very cross, they left shortly after.

I am dreading the summer holidays as children are the worst. It's not their fault bless them, but sadly many times I have had little ones make comments and parents say nothing. I had a lovely experience last summer. I was in the chemist and a little boy said to me why have you got spots? I told him God made me special and he ran to his mum and said "Mummy that lady is special", the mum smiled.

So life has been difficult. I have suffered from depression lots of pain and surgeries, too many to count. A couple of years ago I had to have my gallbladder out and had completions, one doctor said to me "that's a nasty rash you have there". I asked him how long he had been a doctor and he was mortified, "long enough" he said, my reply, "so you don't know about NF?" I said. Then embarrassed he said "I do but it's rare, I've never see it". Sadly in my life I have come across this many times and students flock to have a look. I don't let them anymore, it's my body. I did have one young nurse ask me if she may use my condition for her case study, she was so lovely she asked and didn't assume, I helped her all I could bless her, I hope she went far.

During my teenage years I became very rebellious; I had several jobs none of which I could settle into as I was slow at learning I eventually got a Job with John Lewis, it changed my life, I went from strength to strength I became a cashier which I enjoyed tremendously. I vowed I would continue and eventually I became chief cashier of a small Tesco's. I loved it, I was at last in charge and not being spoken down too. From there I got an assistant manager's job at a newsagent and progressed to manager. I was always respectful and kind to my staff and never expected them to do anything I wouldn't do myself. Once I was mopping the floor and someone came over and said "I will do that Mandy you go and sit down", how lovely and touched I felt.

I went on to marry and have one daughter who was checked until the age of six and was classified cleared. Sadly my daughter and I have parted company but before she left she was showing signs of NF1 but refused to see anyone. My marriage ended and I moved to Devon. I decided to study with the Open University where I gained a degree in Health and Social Care and I also gained a High diploma in counselling.

I had loads of support and was at last able to say to the world I AM NOT THICK, I AM NOT STUPID. Please everyone don't give up there is always a way to get help, if I did it you can too. I am now doing voluntary work as a counsellor. None of my clients have ever asked me about my condition, thankfully they see past my lumps and bumps and see the real Mandy.

More recently I have had surgery to have some fibromas removed and I am waiting to see if I can get funding to have laser treatment on my face, as where I live it's not available on the NHS. I had to go through a process which made me cross and sad but I thought I deserve this it's my life and worth fighting for.

Last year while helping to set up a support group in the south west the local paper printed my story and later on *Chat* magazine printed an article. I have had some varied feedback mostly good one stands out in my mind the most. I was in Tesco in Exeter and a lady asked me if was the lady from the paper, I told her yes waiting for a rebuff but to my surprise she put her arms around me and gave me a hug and said "bless you for being brave" she left me with tears in my eyes.

I am not saying life is perfect for me. I have really down times but I am lucky enough to have a wonderful doctor who gently points out what I have achieved.

If you are reading my story please try not to give up hope, it won't be a walk in the park but you can do it. I was in my 50s when I qualified and I am proud of what have achieved.

By: Mandy Debarring

My Story By: Megan

My name is Megan Michelle Brashares. I am 25 years old.

I was diagnosed with NF at the age of three or four years old and I am the only one in my family that has NF.

I am currently involved with Special Olympics and have competed in rhythm gymnastics, basketball, softball, snowboarding, and snowshoeing. I have been involved with Special Olympics for, I am going to say five years, and I love it.

NF doesn't stop me from doing stuff. I have a boyfriend and he loves me for the way I am. I have pain in my hand. I am the eldest of six kids and none of them have NF. I love children and I am great around children with special needs; I myself have special needs. I am very good with children that are autistic, they communicate with me very well. I want to help with children with special needs someday.

Thanks for reading my story.

By: Megan Michelle Brashares

My Story By: Noreen

My name is Noreen Steenson. I have NF1 and I have had it all my life. I am 39 years old and I have had many surgeries. I am getting more surgery on my hand on 2nd September. I just take each day as it comes. No one else in my family has this condition. With NF1 I have the NF tumours all over my body – from head to toe. The tumours are on the soles of my feet and they are very sore. Sometimes it is hard to walk far but I am one of the lucky ones, there are people with NF1 worse than me so I am glad not to have the problems that these people have.

Another problem I have is learning difficulties but I just do my best all the time. At the moment, I live on my own with my dog Becks, he is a Yorkshire terrier and great company.

My mum passed away three years ago this Christmas. I have two sisters, Kerry and Roisin, and one brother, Declan – all of whom are supportive of my condition. I have good family and friends who look out for me.

When I am out people constantly staring at me make me very sad and I do cry but I have had this all my life. For the last 12 years I have attended a Day Centre. No one there looks at me differently because we are all different and it is where I feel very safe, where I can just be myself and I am glad of the support. I have made lots of good friends with NF from around the world through NF Forums. In 2003 I wrote a poem in a class I was doing in the centre and I got it published on the BBC Skill-wise site – I also won prizes for it, so here it is:

NF

I have NF as you can see.
Tumours all over my body you see.
The pain inside is hard to bear.
But I get through each day as it comes.
I know God above is looking out for me.

He knows what I feel each day that comes.
Never let people put you down
or let anything hold you back.

You have all the love you need at home.
People at home do understand

That one day they will find a cure
And you will be NF free and you can
Thank God above who watches over you
Night and day.

We all are here for the same reason
to live a long, healthy life and be happy.

©Copyright Noreen Steenson 2003
All rights reserved in all countries and at all times

By Noreen Steenson

My Story By: Dave

I grew up and went to school in the 1950s and 60s, there were no classroom assistants then just a teacher standing in front of a class of 40 children. The teachers tried their best to educate us but with me it didn't work. I needed more attention than others. I couldn't hold a pen or pencil or move it across the page in the direction it should have gone. Playground games were just as bad; I couldn't hit any balls that were bowled to me. Because of this I became the butt of many a joke or prank and was always the last picked for a team at games.

Secondary school was a lot worse. After games we were made to take a shower. My body is covered in lumps, bumps and freckles including my genital regions. I'll leave it to your imagination the names I was called.

I was called slow, backward a dumb when I was younger but it wasn't until 1977 that the reason was discovered in the form of a brain tumour.

The tumour was removed and my life turned around.

Apart from getting married, having children and becoming a grandfather, in 2006 I stood for election in the local council elections and won a seat on Lewisham Council and enjoyed four years as a local politician.

I stood down at the following election as my health has started to get worse.

By: Dave Edgerton

My Story By: Connor

I'm Connor Murphy and I was suspected of having NF at nine months old but it took another four years (when I was five) to confirm it. My NF was from a random mutation making me the first in my family to have it. I consider myself one of the lucky ones. I have a very mild case. I have no visible tumors or neurofibromas, unless you know what and where to look.

Because of my NF I have a tumor on my brain, Lisch Nodes (affecting my eyes), neurofibromas, ADHD, and a slight math disability.

Each year my parents and I would make the two-hour drive from New Jersey to Pennsylvania to CHOP (Children's Hospital Of Philadelphia). There I would get eye exams and see my NF doctor, and get my yearly MRI. I did that for most of my visits. Recently I started to go to a more local Hospital (my mom works as a PT there) for my MRIs, and have started to see a NF specialist in NYC– which is about 45 mins away compared to two hours. I've only had MRIs, so far no surgeries. I was closed about my condition until last summer (2012) when I went to a camp for kids with NF (Camp New Friends) for the first time. The camp made me more confident and open about myself. I started telling my friends, posting on Facebook and Twitter, just trying to get more awareness. I have started a blog with Allison, Logan, Jake, and Dylan whose stories are also featured in this book.

The blog is called The Kids With Spots. We can be found on Youtube, Facebook, Blogger, and Twitter under the same name. On it the five of us will be talking about our daily lives with NF, with our friends as guests every now and then– just being ourselves trying to raise awareness. NF has made me who I am today – I have Neurofibromatosis but it doesn't have me.

By: Connor Murphy

My Story By: Allison

My name is Allison Kempe and I have Neurofibromatosis Type 1. Growing up with NF and going to the doctors on a regular basis was normal because my dad, sister and grandma all had NF. My dad didn't really know much about it until he married my mom even though he had several fibromas removed as a kid. When my parents got married they went to a genetic counselor and my dad's condition was finally given a name, Neurofibromatosis Type 1. They began to learn a lot about NF after that.

My sister was three months old when she was diagnosed. She began to display café-au-lait spots like my dad's and my parents knew she had inherited it. The doctors confirmed it. Five and a half years later, I was born with café-au-lait spots, and was immediately diagnosed with it. Everyone in my family is affected by NF differently but we all consider ourselves very lucky not to have very serious affects. NF affects me with café-au-lait spots, scoliosis and Moya Moya disease.

At age eight I had brain surgery for Moya Moya and at age 14 I had spine surgery for scoliosis. Without the support of my family I might not feel the way I do about my NF but because they have always told me that NF is a part of me and that I am not a part of it, I am proud of my NF and feel that it makes me who I am, through the experiences that I have been through and the knowledge I have gained through my experiences with NF that people without may not have experienced or known.

Like most people with NF I have had regular MRI's (every three to five years). I had one at two and another at seven. That is when they found something "odd" on my MRI scan, or that is how my parents described it to me. In reality I had MOYA-MOYA, but even then it wasn't given that name.

Moya Moya is when an artery in your brain is blocked and oxygen and blood cannot get through. It reaches out like tiny fingers trying to develop new flow and appears like a "Puff of Smoke" on an MRI. At the time of my MRI, my right cerebral artery was 98% blocked putting me at major risk or a stroke and permanent damage. My parents were not happy with the first doctors' advice, who told them to just wait and see what happened, see if I had a stroke. My mom spent the next three months using all her free time to do research on blocked arteries, arterial malformations and other effects of NF. She spent every night searching the internet and reading reports from all over the world that sounded similar to my condition. All the while, I had no idea anything was even wrong. Finally she found the name of an amazing doctor at Boston Children's Hospital, Dr. Michael Scott, a doctor who worked to pioneer the surgery that would later save my life. My mom emailed Doctor Scott during the wee hours of a Saturday night, and by 7:00 am Monday morning she received a reply. He asked to have my MRI scans overnighted to him…and within days, surgery was scheduled. I finally asked my parents what was going on and why I had to see doctors. My parents vaguely and calmly explained to me that the doctors had seen something kind of odd on my MRI and that we were going to go to Boston and I was going to have a surgery to fix what was wrong. If it weren't for my parents calm and nonchalant attitude, I don't think I would have been so calm. I remained calm even as I was wheeled into surgery and waving good-bye to my parents. Little did I know they were falling apart on the inside but maintaining a brave front for me.

At the age of eight I of course did not realize how serious the condition was. It was not until several years later that my parents explained more in detail about everything that happened and all the risks. Through my Moya Moya surgery, I met an amazing boy who had the same surgery by the same surgeon. He and his mom, and myself and my mom became best friends and we travel together all the time.

The same goes for my neurofibromatosis, I feel like through doctors appointments, symposiums, camp and other events I have met so many amazing people that I would not have met if I did not have NF. Camp New Friends has been an amazing opportunity for me. I have been given the chance to meet people just like me, learn more NF and grow into a leadership position. I have always said that NF makes me who I am but it has never stopped me from doing anything I want to do or anything I put my mind to. There are things I might have to work harder at, for example in school because of my ADHD and there are some physical things that are more difficult because of my spine being fused but I will never give up and if there is something I want to do I will work until I accomplish it.

By: Allison Kempe

My Story By: Shardai

I was five years old when I was diagnosed with Neurofibromatosis 1. Little did I know at the time, the impact it would have on me. My first tumor was found under my right breast. It had begun to grow so large it looked as though I had begun puberty, but only on the one side. The doctors didn't wait long before performing the first surgery to remove the tumor. Unfortunately, the tumor was larger than the doctors anticipated and they were not successful in removing all of it during the first surgery. My scars mortified me they made me very self-conscious. They reached high on my chest and stretched into my armpit. I had to search hard for summer clothes to cover everything, and my grandma would sew little pink frilly fabric additions onto my swimsuits to help hide the scars.

I contracted NF from a mutated gene, so being the first in the family with it I had no support from someone who had been through it.

I grew up in a tiny town in Montana of about 200 people and had extremely limited resources and medical care to turn to, so we would drive to Salt Lake City for most of my medical care and checkups. The annual checkups were miserable– doctors examining my body, checking for more bumps. I found it especially hard having to let the doctors look at my chest.

I continued visiting my geneticist each year and once I turned nine he and my parents decided that it was time to try again to remove more of the tumor. My parents did not expect the news they were about to receive while I was in the operating room. In the middle of the operation the doctor went out to the waiting room to discuss his concerns with my parents. Because of the way the tumor continued to grow he was skeptical he'd be able to get all of it and was apprehensive about leaving anything behind. In less than ten minutes my parents had OK'd the decision the doctors made in regards to the course of treatment. The decision was made. Instead of just removing a tumor, they would now be performing a radical mastectomy. They took everything– all of the breast tissue, lymph nodes, and my nipple. I woke from surgery and was counseled about what had happened while I was asleep. Even at nine years old I knew what this meant. Fear rushed through me as I thought about what the future would be like. As if it's hard enough as a young woman growing up going through puberty, but me? With one breast? I was really going to be abnormal. Dressing in the locker room for sport and gym class was impossible without the help of a couple close friends to stand just right and cover me without being obvious while I changed into my sports bra and T-shirt.

To make things worse, puberty was in full force and the left breast started to grow while the right remained flat. Bra shopping was miserable and day of shopping sure to end in tears in the dressing room. The thought of dating terrified me. I felt like I was less of a female because of what I looked like under my shirts. One question repeated over and over in my head, "How will a man ever accept this?" I was 12 by the time we began reconstruction. They began with tissue expanders, and finally placed saline implants when I was 16.

I am now 26 years old and still don't look or feel, "normal". At one point I had myself convinced that maybe I really didn't have NF. I had a pen pals growing up that I found through one of the NF newsletters we used to receive who had to have multiple operations and more than one checkup a year. Though the way NF affected me was quite impactful I still consider myself fortunate. I have only had one other tumor removed since the original culprit spurred the diagnosis and can count on my hands the number of the smaller bumps that grew on my arms.

Growing up with neurofibromatosis was difficult because of what it did to my body, my self-image, and my self-esteem. While I am not married, and still hesitant about the dating world, I have found men who have loved me and helped me to accept and embrace my, "battle" scars. Though living with NF took a lot from me, it also made me stronger. Don't get me wrong, there are days that I curse the disorder, and ask God, "Why me?" But then I remember how strong it has made me, and the ways that it shaped the person I am and simply pray for a cure so that no one else has to go through what those of us already diagnosed have had to go through. I pray for those who have worse cases than what I have– stay strong, and carry on.

By: Shardai Urdahl
Bozeman, Montana

My Story By: Brian

My Name is Brian Kempe I am the father of two girls and one boy, and I have NF1. As a kid in the 60s it was not very well known and I don't remember my doctor EVER using the word Neurofibromatosis. Growing up we knew that I had lumps just like my mom but my parents just referred to them as dollops. In Junior High I had two fibromas removed for cosmetic reasons, I grew tired of people pointing and asking what they were. NF affects me in several ways including: café-au-lait marks, fibromas, and a learning disability.

After I got married, I went for a physical and that was the first time I was given the name Neurofibromatosis. I was sent to a geneticist (along with my wife) to learn more about it. We were discussing having children and wanted to understand more about it. When our first daughter was born, there didn't seem to be any signs of NF, however, around her third month, we noticed very faint café-au-lait spots on her belly. We took her to her pediatrician and the diagnosis was confirmed. We just watched and monitored for the various effects we were taught about but nothing significant developed for quite some time. Five and a half years later our second daughter was born with café-au-lait marks on her torso, so the diagnosis was immediate. Our son, the oldest, is not my biological child and therefore does not have NF.

My daughters have had several difficulties but we still consider them not severe. They don't affect their ability to live a normal life. My oldest had a pectus malformation, which required two surgeries, and a tumor removed from her hip joint. Aside from that, she is a successful college student studying to be a teacher and works full time as a nanny. She does not have any visible fibromas, only café-au-lait marks and soft spots in her skin. My youngest daughter has a very mild learning disability, which primarily affects her ability in mathematics. It does not hold her back as she excels in other areas such as writing, reading, history, etc. She was diagnosed with a blocked right middle cerebral artery at age seven, for which she underwent life-saving surgery. She also had spinal fusion for scoliosis at age 14.

As I mentioned, my mother also had NF. She had many fibromas, which increased with age, extremely high blood pressure, café-au-lait marks and in her late 40s she began having seizures, TIA's, and strokes. In her final years she suffered severe dementia. The idea that there was a name for the 'dollops' (fibromas) on her skin didn't interest her and she was treated for whatever medical difficulty she encountered and moved on with life.

When I was born, I had such a big head that the doctors had to break my mother's tailbone in order to deliver me. As an adult I have seen the doctor a few times and my NF has not progressed much, over all I have a much milder case then my mother and I consider myself lucky all around.

Although we know much more about NF, we still don't think of it as something to hold us back. Like my mom, we treat what needs to be treated and live life to the fullest. We simply have a name for it and a better understanding of difficulties we should be aware of should they develop.

By: Brian Kempe

My Story By: Dylan

I'm Dylan Flores. I am 16 years old and I have Neurofibromatosis Type 1 (or NF 1 for short). I was officially diagnosed with having neurofibromatosis between six to nine months of age. However, I was suspected of having it beforehand due to my family history of NF. Along with me, my mom, grandma, grandfather, and uncle all have it on my mom's side of the family. My sister and everyone on my dad's side of the family don't have it. I consider myself to be one of the lucky ones having no tumors and one very small neurofibroma. What I mainly have are Lisch Nodules (pigment in my eyes) and café-au-laitspots (darker pigment than the rest of my skin). I also have a very slight learning disability in reading. Also at one point I was suspected of having ADHD but the tests came back as negative. I can't read as fast as others or understand what I read as well as other's do in my grade.

When I was younger I used to get yearly MRIs and see my neurologist every year to talk about my NF. I haven't done that for a few years now mainly because of the doctor's schedule as well as my parents thinking I don't need any more MRIs. That does not mean I won't get any more MRIs in my life though. I have also had no surgeries to this point which is another reason I consider myself to be one of the lucky ones. Many of my friends that have NF have had several surgeries.

In the summer of 2009 I tried something new. I found a camp called Camp New Friends. It is one-week sleep away camp for people who have Neurofibromatosis. Before camp I had never met another person who had NF. After my first year there I loved it. I made several new friends and have been going to that camp ever since. They are like my second family at camp. Ever since I started going to camp I have been much more open to telling people about my NF. Before I went to camp I was so shy to tell anybody about NF, now that I have been going to camp for five years I feel more comfortable than ever. Camp has also educated me about my disease so now I know more about it. Now what I am trying to do is to spread awareness about the disease. I along with some of my friends Connor, Jake, Allison, and Logan from camp have been tweeting celebrities about NF as well as start a blog to raise awareness. The name of the blog is Thekidswihspots.blogspot.com. We also have a twitter, Facebook page, and YouTube account underneath the same name. All we want to do is to get it more recognized around the world because it is one of the most common disorders, yet one of the most unknown at the same time.

I am not sad that I have NF because it has made me who I am today and I am proud of that. It is a part of me and it always will be. I have Neurofibromatosis, it does not have me.

By: Dylan Flores

My Story By: Logan

Hi my name is Logan… Most people when they see me they think "Oh just a typical teenage girl, she loves makeup, fashion, hair and her boyfriend" but they are wrong... I'm living with Neurofibromatosis Type 1. It is a genetic disorder.

Does it affect me? Yeah I guess you could say that, but I've learned to live with it. Here is just my brief story.

I'm pretty sure I was diagnosed with it when I was about three/four years old. As the years went by I really didn't understand what it was? I mean what six year old knows all the silly terms the silly doctors say… all I knew is I was different from the other kids? At this point not really mentally but psychically. I didn't look like all the other kids on the playground... I didn't look much different but I was different. I had spots other kids didn't have and I really didn't get why. As I got older and the years went by I started to learn more about it. The silly terms I heard the doctors talk about didn't seem so silly anymore… It all started to make sense in a weird sorta way. But as the years went by I started to see mental changes in myself, I didn't work as fast as the other kids, I didn't grasp all the things others did... I was slower... I learned differently then all of the other children I went to school with it wasn't fair I had to work harder than all the other kids... my grades were dropping fast in about sixth grade I was getting all Fs. I found out I had ADHD from my NF and started taking medication to take care of that issue in my life.

I was the first NF case in my family. My friends and family are all affected my NF, but still I don't feel they truly understand what it's like. It's not hard to live with it, but it's by no means easy. I have a few little, but noticeable tumors in a few places where I get asked about A LOT. But I just ignore it, I know they're not trying to be rude, or mean about it, but it is rather annoying. But as the years go by it bothers me less. So yeah I've had a pretty good road on my NF journey but it definitely hasn't been easy.

By: Logan Balie

This person wishes to stay anonymous

When I was just three months old, my pediatrician noticed that there was a lot of freckling on my body. Because of their size it was predicted that I would have NF. I was officially diagnosed at age five, which is also when we found a benign tumor in my brain. It was (and still is) inoperable, but I did receive radiation therapy when I was about six to shrink it. So far it has not grown back, but we still keep it monitored from time to time. This tumor caused the fluid in my brain to build up, diagnosing me with hydrocephalus.

My condition also gave me problems with my eyes and by the age of 13, I lost peripheral vision in my right eye. I received chemotherapy to shrink that tumor, but about a month later we were informed that chemo would not work for children overten. However, this treatment uncovered a tumor in my abdomen, which could only be partly removed because it was pressing against some pretty important things. This operation cost me half my bladder.

In 2012, we discovered another (small) tumor at the base of my skull, pressing against my brainstem and C1-C2 spinal cord, partially paralyzing me on my right side. I was scared that I was going to be paralyzed permanently but fortunately, my chances were quite small. This too could only be partly removed, as it also was pressing against something important. We also found a tumor in the back of my throat, but since it isn't doing any damage, it's going to be left alone (but closely monitored).

I am now 22 and I am a 2009 high school graduate. Though NF may sometimes frustrate me (because I am spontaneously mutated), I do not let it weigh me down and live my life like I have nothing at all.

By:?

My Story Jacob

Hello, my name is Jacob Haberkamp. I have Neurofibromatosis. It hardly affects me, but it gives me ADD, Epilepsy, a mass on my brainstem, learning disabilities, speech problems, then fibromas and café-au-lait spots.

I'm still a normal teenager; I like comics, music, movies, video games, hanging with friends and all that. I don't let NF hold me back on anything. I love being creative, I write stories every once in a while, I write songs, and I wrote a movie. If you look at someone that has a bad case of it and then me you would think that I did not have it.

I was picked on as a kid for having it. I was bullied all throughout school, from Elementary to 10th grade. I was picked on then but I didn't really care anymore. But now my friends help me and support me because of it. I am just like everyone else. All my friends do what they can to help out with NF. Especially my brother Joey, he goes to a lot of the NF things. He has always and always will try to be there for me. He has helped me through some tough times. My other friends have too but not as much as him.

My mother, Diana Haberkamp is the executive director for NF Midwest. I found out about Camp New Friends because of her. I was scared to go at first but now I love going to Camp New Friends. So I can be with other kids and teens with it. I've been going for nine years, my first year was 2004, I think. I started as a really shy camper who always sat on the top bunk during break time, to now an outgoing counselor who goes out of his way to help people. I'm not afraid of what people think about me. People can think what they want but, if they don't know me they shouldn't judge. I've come to love NF to the point where I would not take the cure if were ever found. It has made me into the person I am today. Without it I wouldn't have the friends I have now. I wouldn't have any of the events to hang out with my NF buddies, any of that. I am not the only person in my family who has it, my sister and dad also have it. My sister had a tumor in her neck so she had to have surgery on it. She can no longer turn her neck. She also has scoliosis. My dad has some outer fibromas.

It can be hard for my sister to reach things and drive because of her height and can't turn her neck. It affects me hardly at all compared to some of my friends at camp and my family. When I started college school got harder for me but I had the option of having extra time for tests, which I did not take advantage of and I regret it because I failed the classes.

When I return to college I will use all opportunities to receive help. I didn't want it because I thought I didn't need it. I'm going to start taking classes for social work and music engineering. I don't really have anything else to say, so I guess I'll just end off here. Thanks for reading my story.

By: Jacob Haberkamp

My Story By: Rhona

My name is Rhona and I was born with Nf. 1 I have a very strong family history of Nf and now two of my children have Nf as well, my Nf has affected me throughout my life as in I was born eight weeks' premature and had problems with my legs until I was seven years old.

I have had multiple tumours removed over the years including 26 lumps from my breasts. Four years ago I developed a very bad flu which developed into a chest infection that I could not shift even after three courses of antibiotics. I went back to the doctor again because I was finding it very hard to take a breath.

The doctor told me that it was my smoking that was causing this and was not very sympathetic and begrudgingly said he would send me for an x-ray, I said that I had never any chest problems with my smoking before and was told well there is always the first time.

I went for my x-ray and forgot about it, a letter came through the post a few days later informing me that they had been trying to contact me urgently as there was a problem with my x-ray, my home phone had been playing up and not picking up my calls.

I was told that I was being referred to a thoracic doctor as a matter of urgency, the appointment was for a few days' later, when I went to see the doctor at the hospital he said "Mrs. Black you have had full blown pheumonia in your left lung and there is your tumour".

I was gob smacked as I had not any real symptoms; the tumour measured 4 x 7 cm at this time and was sent for a CT scan which showed that my windpipe, heart, and lung were affected by the tumour and if it hadn't been found when it was, I would simply not have woken up one day as it was slowly choking me to death.

When I went back to see my GP he instantly apologised for what he had said. I then went to see consultant in the Royal Victoria hospital in Belfast and was told I would be brought in for a biopsy to see the extent of the tumour.

My tumour was solid and scans were sent to Brussels, Alabama, to specialist NF doctors to see what it was, it came back to say that they had never seen an NF tumour this size in a chest wall compromising my organs the way it was,

My GP during at the time I was sick was fantastic as I was in the surgery three or four times a week to be nebulized because of the pressure the tumour was causing in my chest

I had five hours of surgery to remove the tumour, with a cardiothoracic surgeon – the best in his field across the UK– and a vascular surgeon as well. They found another large tumour in my groin after a PET scan and removed it as well. I rewrote the medical books in the process.

I recovered fairly well but over the past year or so my health is going down hill. I have been told that it is possible that I have a phyocromocytoma so will be attending more doctors and surgeons in the near future.

By: Rhona Black

My NF Story By" John

Born in 1961, diagonsed with NF age 11 in 1972.

I had 11 shunts put in my head over three years to relieve pressure, so they thought, then they sent me too the MAYO clinic in Minneoastoa for a CAT scan in 1976. They found a cyst on the back of my heart which they removed during Xmas vacation from my freshman year of high school, and that finally solved the pressure issue.

All this caused great issues for my family and myself, but with support from family, friends, teachers and GOD I made it through high school and college. The last 16 years I have worked full time with WALGREENS. I have always worked in retail and in resorts in Colorado Florida and Wisconsin. Take care. GOD BLESS.

By: John Miller

My NF Story By: Bonnie

Hello my name is Bonnie Hathaway, I was born 6th July 1998, I go to Ridgewood school in Doncaster where I am in my last year and I am currently doing my GCSEs.

I was diagnosed with neurofibromatosis when I was about three months old. I got my NF off my mum but my mum's dad or mum didn't have NF, so I guess it was just unlucky for my mum.

I have a few lumps on my stomach but they are not that big. NF does affect me in some ways as I struggle with school, I believe that most people with NF struggle with maths which is what I struggle with the most. I am OK at English and I am not that bad at my science work, but I do struggle as I get confused and everything gets jumbled up in my head, then I get mad with myself because I can't do something.

I also have scoliosis, which is a curvature of the spine. I was admitted to Sheffield hospital when I was about five when my mum noticed my back didn't look right so she took me to the doctors and then they said I would have to go to Sheffield Hospital, that's when I met Mr. Breakwell and he sent me for x-rays and then I found out I had scoliosis. It took about four hours to fit the brace. I went home that night, I was in pain as I was wearing the brace, but then my pain just went away and I got used to it. I had to go to school the next morning, my school said as none of my school tops would fit over the brace I could just wear a baggy top. Everyone was really supportive of me.

A while back know I got to stop wearing my brace. I went into Sheffield hospital with a 28 degrees curve to my spine and it is now 15 degrees and 10 months out of brace.

I am now working towards finishing school with good grades so I can make it into collage to do health and social care. I would like to help others just like Sheffield hospital helped me.

By: Bonnie Hathaway

My Story By: Tina

My name is Tina Sepulveda and I have NF1.

While growing up us girls were told that we had the elephant man's disease.

When I got pregnant the first time was when I found out. I have had a miscarriage (don't know if related).

When I turned 30 all heck broke loose. I started having severe migraines then seizures, now my migraines are daily, seizures whenever they come. I have broken all my teeth out; broke right clavicle, now I don't have one; two broken wrists and many, many, many falls. I've gone through traumas I don't wish on anyone.

This disease is painful to me. It hurts and I can't explain unless you have seen it or been though it. My thoughts and prayers are to all.

My family members have died as a result of NF1. I wish I could find a companion dog again. Nobody can take Jeni's place.

Thank you.

God Bless and Oceans of Love.

By: Tina Sepulveda

"Thank You"

I would like to say "Thank You" to everyone who shared his or her story in my book. One day there will be a cure for NF.

With Love

Kirsty Ashton M.B.E xxx

What is Neurofibromatosis?

Many people will have never heard of neurofibromatosis, yet alone try and say it. But most people have heard about Muscular Dystrophy or Cystic Fibrosis yet, around 25,000 people in the UK are affected by NF. In fact, Neurofibromatosis (NF for short) is as common as Cystic Fibrosis. Why, you may wonder, is it possible that there is a disorder that affects so many people and yet there is still so little known about it?

A disorder that can occur in any family, it affects males and females of all ethnic groups. Nf1 affects one person in every 4,000 births worldwide. It frequently leads to specific learning difficulties and behavioural problems, affects the body's vital nervous system and can lead to serious complications and, occasionally, even premature death. Well, like everything else about neurofibromatosis, it isn't simple to say what life holds or what will happen next.

There are two different types of neurofibromatosis.

Neurofibromatosis type 1, and neurofibromatosis type 2, which I refer to as NF1 and NF2. I am going to talk about NF1 as that is the type of NF that I suffer from.

NF1 is so varied in its effects, and no two people are affected in the same way.

NF1 is a genetic disorder mainly of the nervous tissue. It can cause benign tumours to form on nerve tissue anywhere in or on the body at any time. The signs of NF1 are café au lait marks on the skin, or pale coffee coloured patches. Most people have one or two of these marks but if there are more than six by the time the child is five years old, it is a sign that the child probably has NF1.

Another sign is freckling in unusual places for example, under the armpits, or in the groin area and as a child gets older, tumours (lumps) may start to appear, sometimes just one or two, sometimes lots and lots.

Some of these lumps are soft and can look purplish in colour while others look and feel like peas (I don't mean they are green, just the size) and these can range from being quite small to being really large in size. These benign tumours are always unpleasant and can be disfiguring, even if they are not immediately apparent on the face or exposed areas. The effect on personal relationships and your self-esteem can be affected.
Painful tumours or those that occur in an awkward place can often be removed surgically. But there is always a chance that they will grow back as I have experienced myself after having a tumour removed from my chin that grew back after two years.

What are the signs and symptoms of NF1?

If neurofibromatosis were just a skin complaint, it would have remained a disorder known only to dermatologists and plastic surgeons. But it is much, much, more than just a skin complaint and the complications associated with the NF1 can cause serious problems. The most common of these complications are specific learning difficulties and behavioural problems. But not all children with NF1 have these problems and most have a normal

IQ and are outwardly bright and lively but, at school, they may have particular trouble with reading, writing and math's. Unless NF1 is diagnosed early and the appropriate action taken, these children may never reach their full potential.

Having a learning disability does not mean that you are not intelligent. Having a learning disability means that the person has some kind of trouble with a particular subject, which can take many forms, some people may have trouble remembering instructions, paying attention, difficulty reading or difficulty doing maths.

Learning disabilities can vary from person to person with NF1, but it is important to realise that learning disabilities generally do not get worse over the years.

If you think your child may be struggling in school take steps to deal with it as soon as possible.

Unfortunately, some children with learning disabilities are misunderstood in school, and it's thought they are just being naughty or not working hard enough. Talk to your child and listen to what your child is telling you, don't go pushing your child to work harder without first finding out if they have a problem. Many teachers and parents will push the child to work harder, not realising that the child is working as hard as he or she can. There is nothing stopping a person with learning disabilities from going on to college or even university.

The sooner you pick up on the problem the sooner you can get help for your child.

I struggled at school with spelling and grammar and I

still do. I have been told that I have dyslexia. But it did not stop me from going to college and then on to University and even writing two books, I have had help with my grammar but I guess what I am trying to say is, don't give up, follow your dream and don't let NF stand in your way.

Some people with neurofibromatosis will have other complications associated with NF1, which include high blood pressure, curvature of the spine (scoliosis), benign skin tumours called Plexiform Neurofibroma, internal, spinal and brain tumours (usually benign), speech problems, increased risk of epilepsy and hearing defects all of which can lead to serious difficulties for those affected.

Another sign of NF1 are Lisch nodules. These are very small brown marks that are found on the coloured part of your eye (iris). Over 90 per cent of people with NF1 will have these marks (my mum has these marks on her iris). These marks do not cause any sight problems, but they can be helpful in helping doctors to know if someone has NF1.

Anyone can have a child born with NF1 and that child could be seriously affected by NF1. The reason for this is that NF1 is caused by the mutation of a gene on Chromosome 17. This is no one's fault, it just happens. But if someone with the disorder marries someone unaffected by NF1, there is a 50% chance that each child they have will be born with NF1, depending on whether fertlisation occurs with or without the defect as the faulty gene will be present in half of the eggs or sperm of someone affected by NF1. However, even if the parent with NF1 is only mildly affected, there is no way of predicting how seriously affected any of their children will be. Their child may have some serious complications, or may be relatively unaffected; there is no recognised pattern of the disorder and no predictions can be sure as to what the future holds for each individual in the light of how severely the parent is affected. In my case I have NF1 much worse than my mum does.

In 1991, a huge step forward was made and the gene causing NF1 was found, and an effective treatment is now a realistic hope. I am sure I am not alone when I say "I am looking forward to that day".

After a person with NF1 reaches puberty, small lumps known as peripheral neurofibromas begin to grow on the nerves in the skin. Occasionally they will also grow on nerves that are found deeper in the body. These deeper lumps are called plexiform neuromas and about 50 per cent of people with NF1 will have these. The small lumps can vary in size and shape. Some may be firm and others softer. They can grow as the person gets older.

For some people NF1 is not much more than a skin condition and they may have no idea that they even have NF1. However, for others the lumps can put pressure on the nerves as they grow and cause various problems. If large tumours are close to the surface of the skin, they can be unattractive and may be painful if they are knocked.If lumps are deeper inside the body, they can affect the way the organs in your body function. Rarely, do the tumours turn into cancer. Sometimes the bigger Plexiform may turn cancerous. If you have a tumour that changes, grows, gets hard or becomes painful you should see your doctor and tell him/her that the tumour has changed and is giving pain.

How I learned to cope:
My Mum found out she had NF when she was ten years old; she had no idea why her body was covered in coffee coloured birthmarks or why she had small lumps under her skin.

When mum reached the age of ten, one of the lumps caused her to visit her GP due to the lump giving her some pain. The doctor assured my gran (mum's mum) the lump was nothing to worry about, but as mum and gran were going out of the door the doctor asked if mum had any brown marks on her body, to which my gran said "Yes, loads on her back". Mum was then sent to the hospital to have a biopsy done on the lump and it was at this point mum discovered she was suffering from Neurofibromatosis (NF1). The hospital doctor told my gran that my mum had Von Recklinghausen's Disease, which is what it was called back in the 1960s and that it was hereditary. Gran said that no one on her side of the family had NF1, but looking back mum's dad may have had NF1 as he had small lumps all over his face, head and hands.

Gran divorced from Mum's dad when Mum was only a baby and when Gran contacted him to ask if he had Von Recklinghausen's Disease, and to explain that his daughter had just been diagnosed with the condition and that doctors asked if they could have a word with him, he refused and said that he didn't have it and would not help the doctors. Gran never spoke to him again after that. Over the years Mum's had a few small nodules and some larger lumps, called neurofibromas under her skin removed due to them giving her some problems. Mum said the tumours she has now can give her some pain, and if she knocks them the pain is excruciating. Nearly 40 years ago, very little was known about NF1.

With me if the lumps grow so much that they are severely affecting my nerves and giving me pain, an operation is performed, which gradually cuts them away. I have lost count of how many such operations I have had. I just hope the lumps do not grow back, which they can. I have six- monthly checkups to monitor my condition with an NF doctor. My mum only sees the NF doctor once every two years, and there was talk of my mum no longer being seen, but I don't think this is such a good idea as I know my mum gets in a lot of pain due to some of the tumours and I think anyone who suffers from NF should have the right to be kept an eye on. I hope the doctors change their mind and continue to see my mum and my mum can always see the NF doctor when I am being seen anyway.

People say to me, how do you cope? I say, you just have to get on with things. I ignore it and try to shut it out and get on with life. That's the way I handle it. I may have NF but NF does not have me and I'm pleased to say my brother does not have NF.

Treatment and therapy
There is no cure for NF but the Neurofibromatosis Association is optimistic that there will be an effective treatment within the next five to ten years.

Sometimes surgery may be necessary to remove some tumours (such as acoustic neuromas or brain tumours) and this can cause complications such as facial paralysis.

Medical follow up for NF1
NF1 can cause life-threatening problems, but fortunately these are rare. The majority of people who have NF1 go through life with very few medical problems, which are related to NF and enjoy a good healthy lifestyle.

But it is important to have regular medical follow-up, in order to catch any of the health problems that NF can bring as early as possible.

It is a good idea, to see a doctor who is familiar with the disorder at least once a year or more often if a particular problem is spotted. The doctor can be your family doctor or may be a specialist who deals with neurofibromatosis.
You should use these visits to ask any questions you might have about the condition, and to talk about any changes you have noticed in your body. It is especially important to tell the doctor if you are in pain, experiencing numbness or tingling noticed sudden growth of any of your Neurofibromas, getting headaches, or noticed any new neurofibromas.

Usually, your doctor will be able to reassure you with a simple examination. Sometimes the doctor may request special tests to be done to check out any symptoms you may be experiencing. This is important in order to catch problems as early as possible.

Whether you've got NF or not, it can be alarming to find a tumour. There's no point worrying in silence, so check out any changes with your doctor and, remember, many tumours turn out to be benign and harmless. Even in awkward places, so it's important to keep an eye on tumours and see a doctor regularly to check they're not turning nasty.

Help and support for NF sufferers:
Most signs of NF1 appear during childhood or adolescence, and signs of Nf2 appear during the 20s.

Discovering you, or someone you know, has got NF can be a bit of a shock, but there is help and support available for NF sufferers in the UK. Organisations such as the Neurofibromatosis Association can provide help and information about the condition.

Couples with a family history of neurofibromatosis who are thinking of having a baby can be referred to a genetics specialist before getting pregnant, for advice.

However, neurofibromatosis is unpredictable, how mild or severe a parent's case is has no bearing on how the child will be affected or what complications they may have.
Unfortunately there's still a lot we don't know about neurofibromatosis. It's an unpredictable condition, there's no way of knowing exactly how it will develop for you, and how your café au lait patches will look in coming years.

There isn't any medical or surgical treatment that can cure or reverse the condition. In fact, a major focus of research is to try and develop effective therapy. The best that doctors will be able to offer at the moment is to keep a close eye on you and look out for any signs of complications.

It is normal to feel angry and overwhelmed at times as you face the uncertainty that NF brings. You must learn to live your life, and not let NF rule your life. The more you understand about the condition the more you will be in control, so be sure to ask questions of your parents, teachers, and medical professionals. Find someone you trust, and share your feelings, fears and frustrations with them. The challenges posed by having NF are hard, but they can be overcome.

If you have recently found out that you or a member of your family has NF, please don't worry, I'm here to help and support you in any way I can. You may feel you are alone right now, but you're not.

Please go to my web address at www.kirstysstory.co.uk and send me an e-mail and I'll get back to you as soon as possible. If you or somebody you know suffers from Neurofibromatosis don't worry. Together we can help each other.

Some pictures showing signs of NF

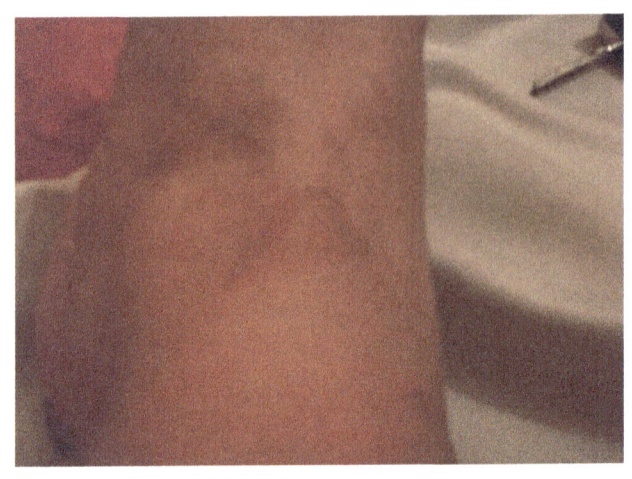

A brown café-au-lait mark on my foot and neck, having six or more of these marks is an indication that you have NF.

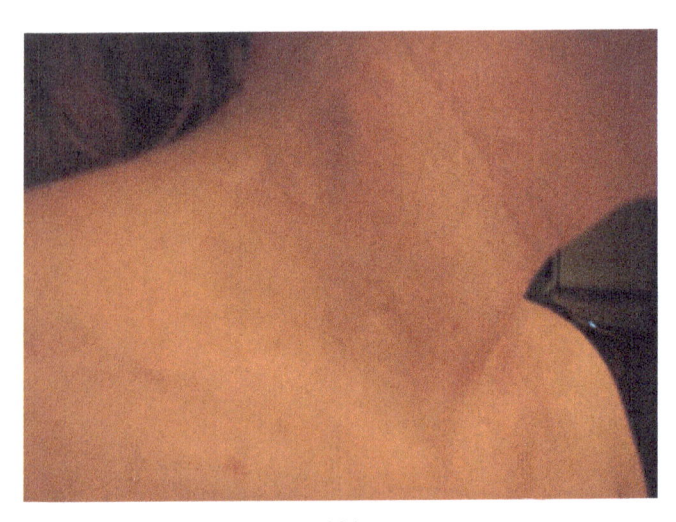

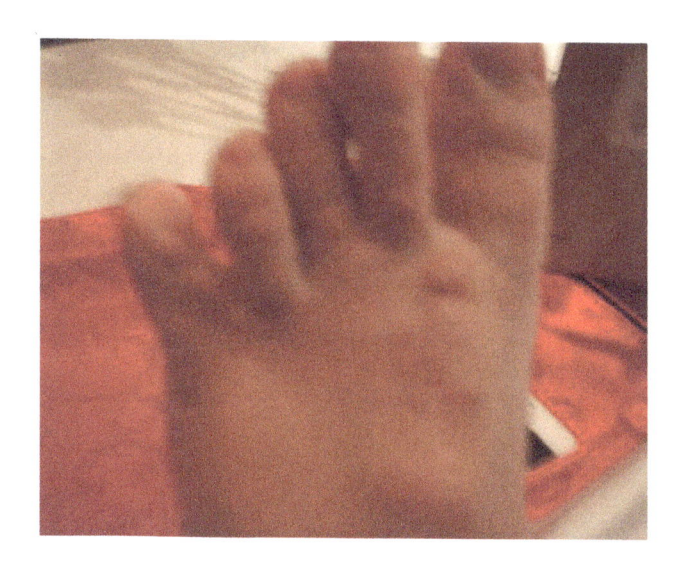

NF tumours can grow on any nerve. Above: some tumours on my foot, and below: one on my mum's toe.

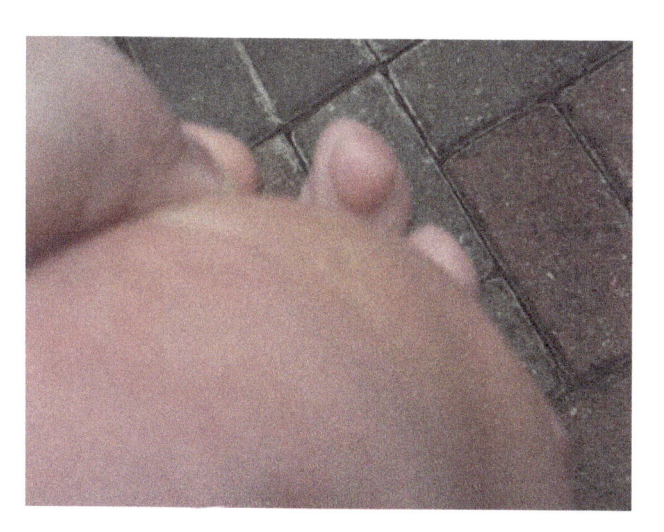

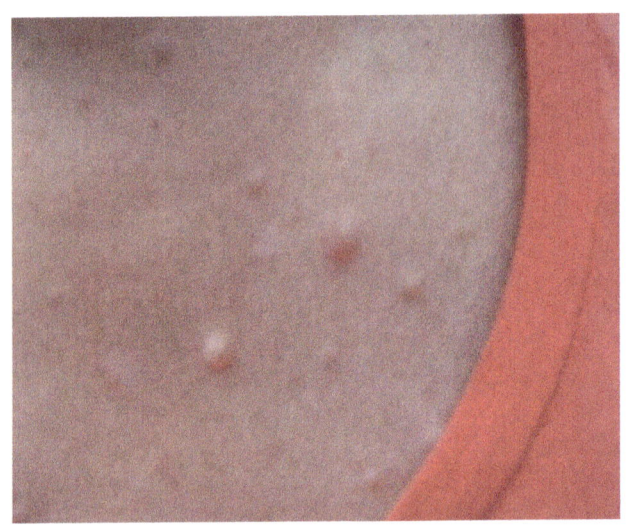

This is what some of the tumours look like that grow on the chest and stomach, they are only small but they can give a person a lot of pain if they have any straps that rub on them.

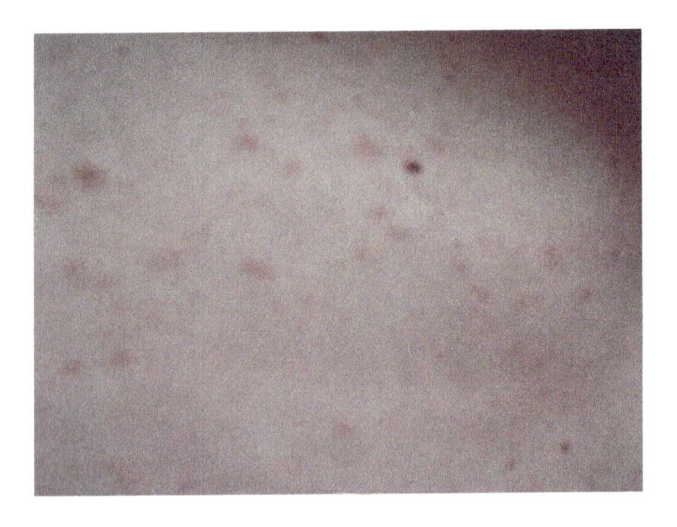

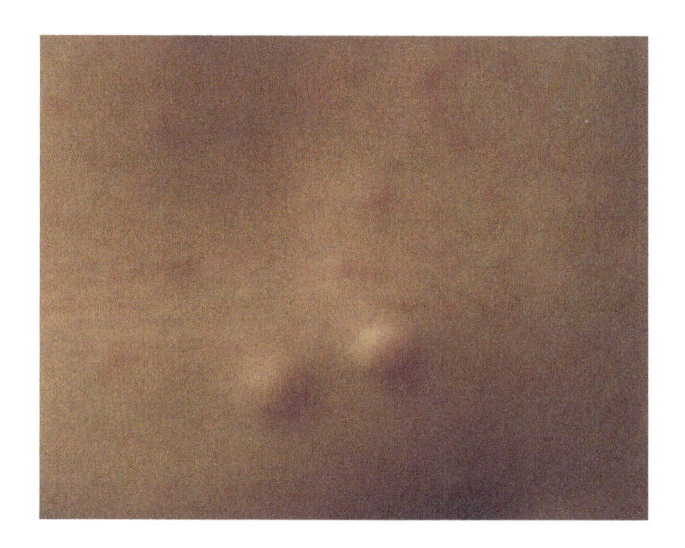

The NF tumours can grow to any size and it does not matter how big they are they can still cause a lot of pain and discomfort. These tumours are on my mum's back.

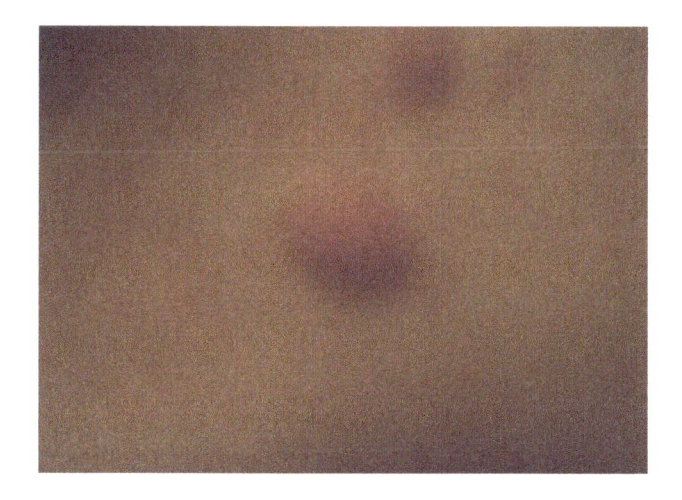

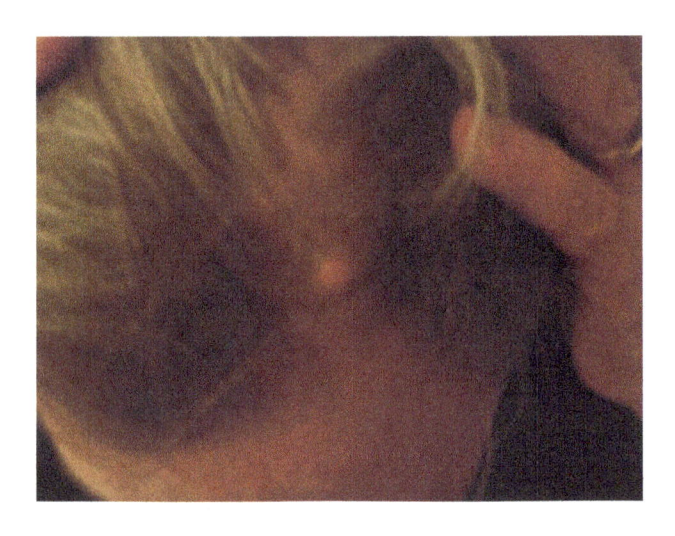

They also grow on the scalp; unfortunately these tend to bleed when you catch your hairbrush on them. Below: my leg after three tumours were removed.

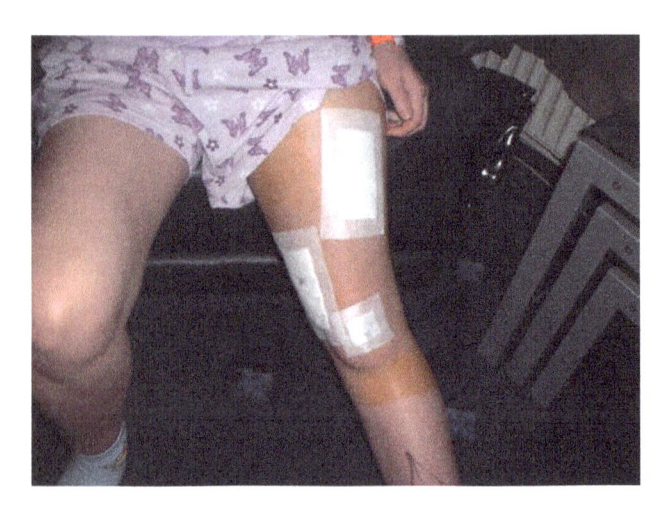

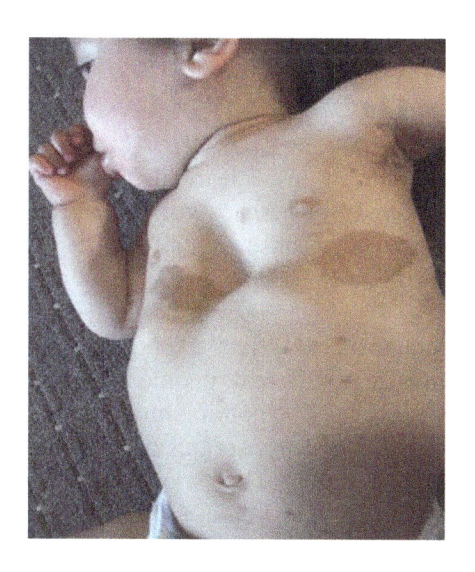

You can clearly see that Elli's chest dips in, and the brown café-au-lait mark on Little Elli's chest.

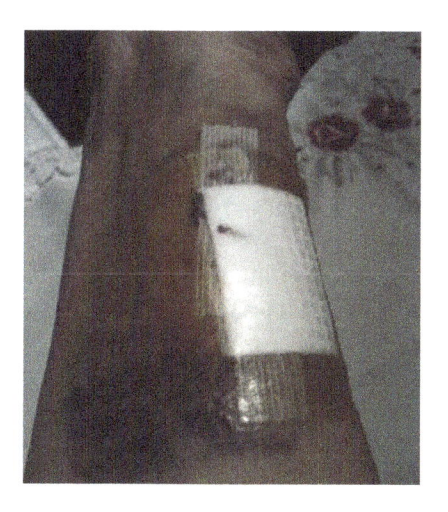

This is my mum's arm after she had one small tumour removed that was giving a lot of pain.

Neurofibromatosis Question and Answers

You may have just learned that you have neurofibromatosis, or perhaps you have been going to doctors for years because of the disorder and living with more serious complications.

Neurofibromatosis can affect the body in many ways, and it can affect different people in very different ways. In some it may be nothing more than a nuisance, but for others it can cause serious medical problems. It is natural to have lots of questions when a person is told that he or she has a condition such as neurofibromatosis.

Below are some of the questions that I have been sent over the years; I hope these answers help you if you have NF.

Q: Does NF remain stable over a lifetime or does it get worse as we get older?
A: NF1 and NF2 are both progressive disorders, but the rate of progression and any complication are very much unpredictable. A person with NF1 may experience an increase in the number of neurofibromas that they have over his or her lifetime.

Q: Is there a cure for NF?
A: The simple answerer is "NO", but there are researchers worldwide working to find more effective treatments that will help people with NF.

Q: Is there any research being done for NF?
A: Yes, research is being carried out all the time.

Q: Is NF the same condition as the Elephant Man had?
A: No, but for many years doctors believed that Joseph Merrick (the elephant man) had NF, then in 1986 it was proved that Joseph Merrick had an extremely rare condition called Proteus Syndrome and not NF.

Q: Does NF occur more in men or women?
A: NF affects both women and men of all races equally.

Q: Can someone with NF still donate blood?
A: Yes, people with NF can donate their blood, and anyone who receives their blood will not develop NF.

Q: Is NF an inherited condition only?
A: No, 50% of cases of NF will have been inherited from a parent who has NF. The other 50% of NF cases are a result of a spontaneous mutation in the sperm or egg cell.
A person affected by NF has a chance of passing the condition on with every pregnancy they have.

Q: If I think or someone I know may have NF what should I do?
A: for anyone who thinks they may have NF they should first see their family doctor who will then put them in contact with a doctor who is more knowledgeable about NF who will then discuss your symptoms and concerns with you.

Q: what is the difference between NF1 and NF2?
A: if two or more of the following are present, a diagnosis of NF1 is normally confirmed.

- Family history of NF1

- Freckling under the arms or in the groin area
- Six or more light brown café-au-lait marks on the skin (these look like birth marks)
- Small pigments on the eye's iris, which are called lish nodules
- Small bumps (neurofibromas) on the skin
  Skeletal abnormalities, such as bowing of the legs, curvature of the spine (scoliosis)
- Optic Glioma

With NF2 if one or more of the following are present a diagnoses of NF2 is likely.

- Family history of NF2
  Tumours found on both the auditory nerves, which may cause deafness, balance problems or ringing in the ears
- Tumours can be found on the brain, meninges or spinal cord
- Pre-senile cataract

Q: What is the prognosis for someone with NF?
A: in most cases the symptoms of NF1 are mild and the person can live a productive life. But in some case, however, NF1 can be very debilitating and unfortunately no doctor can say how you may be affected by the NF.

Q: Should I tell my child teachers that my child has NF? I don't want my child to be labelled as having a learning disability.
A: Yes, it's always advised that you tell your child teachers that your child has NF as this will help to lead to earlier detection and treatment of any learning problems your child may have due to NF. It is very important to recognise learning disabilities and to take

steps to deal with them as soon as possible. Unfortunately some children with learning disabilities are misunderstood in school, and thought to have bad behaviour, or not be working hard enough. Some teachers may try and push the child to work harder, not understanding that the child is working hard, but they are just unable to perform certain task as well as they can others. A person with NF can go on to college and even university with the special help and support they need.

Just remember you are not alone. I welcome everyone who visits my website and I look forward to many new friendships and helping many more people with this unpredictable and cruel condition.

Cassie Gunn Asked:

Q: When you were a child did you understand fully what NF was?
A: I understood as much as I needed to in basic terms, this is why the website was developed to help other young children understand about it in a simple way. I knew I had lumps and bumps that grew and if they hurt I would tell mummy and daddy, I would say I was about nine when my spine went on me that I fully understood.

Q: What was it like to be in hospital for three months?
A: It was not nice at times, but I always think positive I had lots of friends that came to see me all the time and that helped me recover. I did not like being in and being away from my gran and brother though, and I felt bad for my brother as mum was with me all the time. I did not mind being in hospital though as I knew

it was to make me better and I understood this.

Q: Did it ever bother you going to and from hospital all the time?
A: No, not really, it was a day off school, and I had lovely ambulance drivers that would take me, so I enjoyed my visits and I got to meet lovely inspirational people as well.

Q: Have you ever been bullied for having Nf?
A: Yes, but mainly though my braces and my scoliosis, as I was different and that's how I was seen.

Q: Do you wish you didn't have NF?
A: No, it does not bother me. If I had never had NF I would not be the person I am today.

Q: Did you miss not being in school five days a week like other kids?
A: No, not really, I don't think I noticed it that much.

Q: What was it like seeing Peter Andre in the flesh? Lol
A: Wished it could have been longer, gutted there was security there, maybe he had security as he knew I liked him lol. I am just so appreciative of Kelly for arranging this with the Forum in Romiley and Peter for giving up his time to talk to me.

Q: What does it feel like to be a true inspiration?
A: I don't think I am, I am just doing what I can to help others.

Q: What is your favourite girls' and boys' name?
A: If I have children the boys would be called Oliver, Taylor, Reece, and if I have a girl it would be, Brooke,

Q: What was your favourite childhood cartoon?
A: Brum, Recess, Rugrats, everything Disney related.

Q: Who is your idol?
A: People that I meet that inspire me – Peter Andre, is amazing.

Q: What is your pet hate?
A: Chavs, and people that are disrespectful and judgmental.

Q: What is your favourite food/drink?
A: Pizza, spicy curry, and I drink coffee, red bull – basically the things that I am not allowed lol.

Q: Who was your first crush?
A: Chris Wilson, I was in primary school and liked him all the way through and into high school. When I was in high school it was Steven Crane.

Q: Apart from needles what other fears do you have?
A: Wasp, bees, and being in a relationship, as I don't want to get close to someone in case I get hurt.

Q: Do you think it is weird you and me were both born 5.4.90 and we both have Nf and scoliosis and have the same interests?
A: No, I think its fate, it's like you're a sister. Well, it's what I see you as anyway.

Q: what season do you like best?
A: Summer – as it helps my pain.

Q: What was it like being in the USA?
A: Incredible, I love it there, everyone is so welcoming and lovely, I would move there tomorrow. My pain is

eased due to the weather and I am more happy and relaxed. People don't judge me.

Q: Who is your favourite pop star?
A: I do not really have a favourite pop star, I have favourite bands I like but I am more about the music than the person... Twin Atlantic, Simple Plan, Blink 182, Greenday, 30 Seconds to Mars, Michael Buble, McFly, Daugtry.

Q: What's the most amount of money you have spent on a teddy bear?
A: You really don't want to know, if where talking about in one go it is $300, bought a teddy, dressed him, then I bought him a car, a bed, sleeping bag, LOL.

Q: Can you sing?
A: I would call it singing, others would differ.

Q: Have you ever felt embarrassed about having Nf?
A: Nope.

Q: What made you want to write a book?
A: I just wanted to help out as many people as possible.

Q: What other famous people would you like to meet?
A: Simon Cowel (for my mum), Peter Andre again, so I can have a proper conversation, not like I want to woo him or anything, and Lord Alan Sugar.

Q: Who do you admire?
A: My gran.

Q: What does your family think of what you have done?
A: They are happy and proud, I think.

Q: You could be any animal what would you be?
A: Not 100% sure, maybe a cheetah because they're really fast and I have never run properly before so would like to give it a go, but I am more of a monkey/dolphin person.

Q: If you won the lottery what would you do?
A: I would invest it for a few months, whilst I get over the shock of winning, and then I would sort my family out and get myself a nice 4-5 bedroom house so that I could foster and adopt children; build my music studio in my room; sort very close friends out, and of course `Wish Upon a Star', like secure the money for Centre Parcs for a few years, and sort the camps out for CWT.

Bonnie Marie Asked:

Q: Do you ever think to yourself you wish you and your mum never had this condition?
A: I wish that we did not have to go through the pain and treatment as I would not wish ill health on anyone and if I could take it away I would. But if I never had it we would not have met the people we have and gained true friendship.

Q: Do you think well there are always people worse off than us with NF and scoliosis?
A: There's always somebody worse off than ourselves. I am an optimistic person I see the glass half full and it's the way I live my life.

We are all going through pain and suffering and probably all have experienced the same problems as each other, but we are there for people and can support each other. Some people are not as lucky to have the friendship we do and the support.

<u>Debra Merrington Asked:</u>

Q: Saw your post re: questions for your new book (loved the last one by the way; read it on my Kindle). Wanted to ask what your organisational skills were like, ie. tidying up, keeping things in the right place and getting things done on time.

A: I have always tried to be a clean and tidy person, growing up I have my days where I misplace things and my room is a mess, I prefer clutter as I seem to find things better as I can see it. But if it's a clean, yes, it's easy to go round my room and stuff mobility wise but it's annoying as I can't find anything and then it stresses me out. I do have memory issues big time, it's why I prefer to keep out things I need like paperwork, etc.

Q: Also, do you ever feel like you don't fit it with people? I often feel quite 'odd' not as socially adept as most people, (but I do have friends and get on well with most people) though I've always worked with children and at times in positions of authority so I'm certainly not un-intelligent and fortunately didn't experience the specific learning difficulties my daughter does. Maybe these social difficulties are not connected to NF. I'm taking part in a survey with St Mary's about what it's like living with NF.

Thanks, Deb x

A: I have understood and known from an early age I am different and unique and I won't fit in everywhere;

not everyone fits in. I was not that popular in school until I became poorly and then everyone wanted to be my friend. I have realised over the years, and mainly this year, who my friends are, (not online) it is not many, but it's enough, I know they're here for me and I am there for them, and they live all over the country. I wish I could fit in more with people, but I feel it is because they don't understand my condition and the problems it can cause, so I am seen as wired and different, and going out in braces and on crutches with good-looking people is like I affect their image, so I think that's a reason why.

<u>Anonymous</u>

Q: Is it possible to know whether my child has NF1 without doing genetic testing?
A: Definitely – in fact, NF is most often diagnosed clinically, and many patients with NF never undergo genetic testing.

Q: Are neurofibromas contagious?
A: No, not at all. NF1 is a genetic disorder, meaning that if your child has it, it was already in his/her genes when he/she was born. Neurofibromas don't "spread" from person to person.

Q: Can we predict how my child's condition will progress?
A: Unfortunately, NF1 is highly unpredictable. It's very difficult to predict whether your child's symptoms will be mild, moderate or severe. Severe complications are rare.

Q: My child has many café-au-lait spots, does that mean that she will develop very severe NF1?
A: There is no connection between the number of café-

au-lait spots and the severity of NF1.

Q: If my child becomes a parent someday, will her children also have NF1?
A: As with anyone with NF1, there's a 50% chance that his/her child will also have the condition.

<u>**Rachel Walters Asked**</u>

Q: Hi Kirsty my question is it possible for NF to skip a generation as my maternal granddad and his sister had it, no one in my mum's generation has it, I have it, my cousin has it and his two children have it – surely it is not possible to have six spontaneous mutations in one family? Dr Ferner examined my mum and said she does not have NF so I'm confused, thank you x
A: It's extremely unusual for NF1 to skip, but some mutations cause a predominantly internal form with little or no skin pigmentation. The only way to prove it is to find the gene mutation in one affected person then test all the rest. It is certainly possible that all the rest of her family has one mutation (her cousins' parent has mild features) and that she alone represents a new mutation, this is certainly well documented in a number of families.

Rachel's question was answered by: Professor Gareth Evans.

Thank you

For your questions, I hope I have helped you.

Useful NF1 Links

The Neuro Foundation provides the following website links to additional information on their website (www.nfauk.org) and have allowed me to share them with you.

The Neuro Foundation's team of Specialist Advisors each work with over 500 people affected by Neurofibromatosis every year, giving practical, emotional and medical advice.
The links below will hopefully be able to offer further helpful information for people affected by NF1.

However, please note that no responsibility can be accepted by The Neuro Foundation or myself (Kirsty Ashton M.B.E) for the contents of the sites. The Neuro Foundation does not necessarily endorse any of the web links but have provided me with them as a stepping-stone to further information. If you are in any way concerned about your health and NF, it is recommended that you always consult your family doctor.

- Children's Tumour Foundation: **www.ctf.org**
- Contact a Family for families with disabled children: **www.cafamily.org.uk**
- Charity to help children with brain related conditions: **www.cerebra.org.uk**
- Changing the way you face disfigurement: **www.changingfaces.org.uk**
- Charitable organization caring for disabled children: **www.newlifecharity.co.uk**
- Gene test website: **www.geneclinics.org**

- Genetic Alliance UK: **www.gig.org.uk**
- UK Government website: **www.gov.uk**
- Free, independent and confidential advice on benefits, DLA, PIPS's etc.: **www.adviceguide.org.uk**
- Strongbones awards grants for medical equipment: **www.strongbones.org.uk**
- Over the Wall runs residential activity camps for children: **www.otw.org.uk**
- The National Parent Partnership offers information and support to parents and carers: **www.parentpartnership.org.uk**
- Information for parents of children with autism spectrum and other neurological difficulties: **www.cambiangroup.com/Ourservices/EducationServices/ParentalResources.aspx**

What some of my doctors have to say

I asked some more of my doctors to explain some of the medical facts about my condition.

I have also included Mr Neil Oxborrow's (my spinal doctor) and Dr Sue Huson's (my NF doctor) comments from my previous book.

Professor Gareth Evans

Professor Gareth Evans is one of the nicest guys my mum and I have had the pleasure of meeting. Both Gareth and his lovely wife Chris De Winters are lovely people. They are both working hard to set up a camp for children with NF. We all need to help this happen by raising funds for "Children with Tumours".

Neurofibromatosis type 1 and Kirsty

Neurofibromatosis type 1 or NF1 for short is a Cinderella condition, which despite affecting around 1 in 2500 people (there will be an average of one patient for every GP) is not well known or understood either in the medical profession or by the public as a whole. Partly this is because of the huge variability with how people can be affected even within the same family. NF1 is inherited from an affected parent in about half of all situations but a further half are due to spontaneous (new) mutations of the NF1 gene that occurred in the egg or sperm that made that individual. Many people with NF1 hardly know they have the condition, with just pigment marks on the skin and a few minor growths in the skin. However, others can be more severely affected with internal growths affecting the spine and brain that cause pain, loss of function including vision and can on occasion become malignant (cancerous). The tumours in NF1 occur on the nerves and are called neurofibromas but tumours of the brain called gliomas can occur on the nerve to the eye and cause problems in early childhood.

My name is Professor Gareth Evans, I am a professor in genetic medicine and cancer epidemiology at Manchester University and have specialized in neurofibromatosis, publishing 165 papers or chapters on the conditions. I took over running the NF service in 1991 and became aware of a very brave girl who was having major problems relating to her NF1. Kirsty Ashton has had multiple operations for neurofibromas. These have affected her mobility and leave her in almost constant pain. Yet despite this she has been an amazing ambassador for NF, raising money for wish upon a star and a new charity that I am involved with called Children with Tumours. Kirsty's energy and drive are phenomenal with great communication skills and a warm sense of humour despite her NF related problems. Whilst the future of NF1 is in medical hands, the future of NF awareness is in good hands with people like Kirsty. Kirsty has been with Children with Tumours from the start and with her help and drive we hope to make NF a household name with its recognition being developed in a positive and vibrant way.

By: Professor Gareth Evans

Dr Sue Huson
My NF Doctor

I have known D Sue. Huson for as long as I can remember, she is an excellent doctor and sees both my mum and me for our NF. What Dr Sue Huson doesn't know about NF is not worth knowing.

Neurofibromatosis type one (NF1): the genetic condition underlying Kirsty's medical problems Sue Huson MD FRCP, Consultant Clinical Geneticist Neurofibromatosis Centre Regional Genetic Service Central Manchester Foundation Trust.

Neurofibromatosis what's that? It's a real jawbreaker of a word! Said one of my new patient's Dad this week. From a medical perspective we use Neurofibromatosis as an umbrella word for a group of genetic conditions that cause benign tumors to grow on nerves (neuro-). Under the microscope these contain fibrous tissue (fibro-) and multiple tumors may develop (-osis). Kirsty and her Mum have the most common form, type one (NF1), which affects about one in every 2500 babies born. This is as common as Cystic Fibrosis- so why is NF1 not a household name? The reason is that it affects people very differently, even in families, and for many people it is just a skin condition not associated with major medical problems. Even when it does affect people seriously it can do so in many different ways. I have been running an NF1 clinic for nearly 20 years and have only met one or two other people with the combination of NF1 related problems Kirsty has.

What causes NF1?
NF1 is caused by a spelling mistake in one of the genes (called the NF1 gene).

We all have two copies of every pair of genes – we get one from our mum and one from our dad. People with NF1 have a spelling mistake (referred to as a mutation) in one of their NF1 genes. About half the people with NF1 inherit it from their mum or dad. The others are the first people in their family to have NF1 – in them the spelling mistake happened either as the egg or sperm was made or very early in their development. When people with NF1 have children there is a 50:50 or one in two chance of passing it on.

How does NF1 affect you?
I find it easiest to think about this in two ways first, to look at the things that develop in nearly everyone with NF1 and then to look at what I will refer to as NF1 complications, the things that only happen in some people.

The main way NF1 shows itself in children is by flat brown marks on the skin, called café au lait spots (they are coffee coloured and were first described by some French doctors). Some may be present at birth but it is more usual for them to begin to show in the first year or two. All of us can have one or two of these spots but people with NF1 nearly always have more than six. The other main thing that everyone with NF1 develops is the neurofibromas themselves – they are small purplish lumps on the skin. They begin to develop anytime from around ten years of age. The numbers that develop are very variable but when people have a lot they can be a major cosmetic problem. Fortunately they mainly grow on the skin of the trunk so when you meet people with NF1 there are usually no signs you would see when they are dressed.

What makes NF1 difficult?
If all people with NF1 got were the café au lait spots and skin neurofibromas it would be thought of as a skin problem and nothing else. The problem is people with NF1 are at risk of a long list of complications. Most of these can occur in any one of us, it is just that in people with NF1 there is a higher chance. For example, about half the people with NF1 struggle with their learning at school. This is the most frequent complication, the next most frequent are related to more complicated neurofibromas than the small ones on the skin. Some people develop neurofibromas, which grow very large called plexiforms and these can be a major cosmetic problem. Other people develop neurofibromas on the internal nerves and if these cause pressure on the nerve it can cause problems with nerve function.

The other complications all affect far fewer NF1 patients but the list of what can happen is long and can affect almost any part of the body. This causes a real problem for people with NF1 and their doctors – we don't have good ways of predicting how NF1 will affect people and the variability means we can't offer screening tests that will pick up every possible problem. This uncertainty with NF1 is one of the most difficult things about living with it, things can crop up at any time – the chance of bad problems are still small but bigger than they are for other people. The best description I have heard of this comes from a man with NF1 interviewed by Professor Joan Ablon (Ablon 1992) – she spent several years talking to people with NF1 to find out how they coped with the condition.

Most diseases will unfold in a certain way – slower or faster. With NF1, because the symptoms are so unpredictable and variable, you don't know whether there will be symptoms, what they might be, or if they will be serious. You never get your balance or equilibrium how to deal with them. After one thing appears and you deal with it, here comes another. It is not just that there are big and little fires, there is always the worrying sign up that says Danger of Fire. The psychological burden is always there, regardless of the extent of the physical problems...

NF1 and Kirsty
Kirsty's mum has NF1 but for her it has mainly been a skin problem. In turn, Julie had inherited NF1 from her dad but her parents split up when she was only a baby and she doesn't know much about her dad's NF1. Kirsty and Julie show exactly how variable NF1 can be for Julie it has been a skin problem and she has needed a few skin lumps removed from time to time. For Kirsty, ever since her scoliosis was picked up when she was eight NF1 became a bigger issue. The curve of her back gradually got worse and she needed an operation to stop things getting worse at the age of fourteen. It was then that a further problem became obvious – Kirsty is someone whose neurofibromas are growing mainly internally and not on the skin. So while I have known Kirsty we have realised she has them on most of the nerves as they leave her spine and on many of the big nerves in her arms and legs. There is no way these can all be removed without causing major nerve damage and so we have to carefully monitor her and only remove the neurofibromas if they grow particularly big and press on a vital organ like the spinal cord. The tumours Kirsty has are beginning to cause her nerves not to work properly, she has developed weak ankles with foot drop and her knees keep giving way.

The frustrating thing is we have no medical treatments, which will stop this progression. Although

Scientists are working hard to understand NF1 and this work is now identifying drugs which may shrink NF1 tumours, clinical studies are only just beginning. We hope that over the next two decades we will find successful drug treatments for NF1.

How Kirsty copes with her NF1
It is a real privilege to know Kirsty and her mum Julie. Some people faced with severe health problems affecting their mobility and making them easily tired, would have found it easier to "give in" to their NF1 and not do very much. Not Kirsty – every time I meet her there is always some new fundraising venture on the go or she has been talking to someone with NF1 about how she copes with it. Kirsty is a great ambassador for NF1 and for all children with chronic health problems. Keep up the good work!

The information from Dr Sue Huson was first printed in my first book "*Kirsty's Story, Living with Neurofibromatosis and Scoliosis*".

Mr Neil J Oxborrow

My spinal doctor

NJ OXBORROW CONSULTANT SPINAL SURGEON

I have known Mr Neil J Oxborrow for many years. When I was in hospital and he did his ward rounds he would grab my teddy saying I was to old for them (he was only messing), I would pay him back by getting squeaky toys for his dog. He is a really nice guy and very understanding. I would not let anyone else do surgery on my spine.

I first met Kirsty in 2004 by which time Kirsty had already seen enough doctors to more than fill her notes with correspondence. At this time the neurofibromatosis had caused her spine to curve to one side (scoliosis). Scoliosis is quite common in neurofibromatosis and often the curves can progress rapidly. Kirsty had already been seen at this stage by the neurosurgeons as she had pain in her legs from lumps forming on the nerves as they came out of the spine (neurofibromas). It was felt by the neurosurgeons that nothing really could be done for the pain, as they could not be sure which of these lumps was actually causing pain.

We discussed in detail what an operation on Kirsty's spine would mean and decided to proceed. On the 10th March 2005 Kirsty was brought into hospital initially to have an operation on the front of the spine. To gain access to the front of the spine involved making a cut along Kirsty's side and taking out a rib. When we got to the front of the spine we found that it was covered in neurofibromas and the disease was very extensive. During spinal surgery we monitor the function of the spinal cord to make sure that it carries on working well throughout the procedure. Any surgery on the spine carries a small risk that the spinal cord doesn't like what we are doing and at worst this can mean that some patients can lose the use of their legs. This is a very rare complication. Halfway through the operation the monitoring started to suggest Kirsty's spinal cord was not happy. In this situation we do not take any chances at all and we stopped operating, sewed Kirsty up and woke her up. We all breathed a sigh of relief when Kirsty woke without any problems in her legs.

The safest thing to do is to wait a period of time and then take the patient back to theatre to finish the operation. As we had already done quite a lot of the operation at the front and taken out a lot of Kirsty's discs (bits of gristle in between the bones of Kirsty's spine) we thought it simply best to do the second operation from the back rather than go in from the front of the spine. Kirsty was then taken to theatre for a second operation on 25th March 2005.This time everything went without any cause for concern.

Although the spinal side of things was now fine Kirsty had significant problems with sickness after the operation and was really quite unwell with continued nausea and vomiting. This was so bad it meant Kirsty was losing quite a bit of weight. In the end she was transferred under the care of one of the medical doctors for further management until this settled down. Kirsty has continued to get significant back pain after surgery and has also had problems from other neurofibromas affecting nerves in her legs, thighs and really the extent of Kirsty's disease is such that much of this pain and many of these problems are not really amenable to treatment. It is important for us to keep an eye on these neurofibromata to make sure none get particularly big or painful as this can mean this turns into a more nasty form of growth or tumour.

Despite continued pain, Kirsty never ceases to come to clinic with a smile and has had to be banned from bringing presents of squeaky toys for my dog as the noise at home was becoming unbearable.

Her latest pain would be well above the area that was previously operated on and we are currently thinking about whether further surgery may be of benefit. The pattern of Kirsty's pain is very difficult to be sure of, however, as it has always been difficult to know how much of the pain was coming from the neurofibromas, which we cannot do anything about and how much may be coming from something we could do something about.

By: Mr Neil J Oxborrow

The information from Mr Neil Oxborrow was first printed in my first book *"Kirsty's Story, Living with Neurofibromatosis and Scoliosis"*.

**Mr Christopher Duff
(Plastic Surgeon)**

Mr Christopher Duff is a fully trained and accredited Plastic Surgeon working at Wythenshawe Hospital.

My mum and I would not allow any other plastic surgeon to do our surgery now. He is the very best at what he does and is a great guy too. Mr Christopher Duff has helped both my mum and me by removing tumours when they are causing pain and discomfort.

Dr Ilan Lieberman
(Consultant in Pain Management)

Dr Lieberman is my pain consultant and the doctor that I spoke about in my first book. Dr Lieberman is the doctor that wore the wacky ties. He is a really nice guy and when I go to see him we always have a chat about the fundraising that I have been doing.

Dr Lieberman does a lot of charity work too. Both my mum and I see Dr. Lieberman for our pain.

Stephen Shiel and Me

Steve is my Orthotist

Stephen measures and supplies me with all my different braces when I go to Orthotics, like my back brace, knee braces and foot braces. He is a really cool guy and I love seeing picture of his granddaughter, she is such a little cutie. Stephen also provides my mum with her braces.

I first met Kirsty last year in February 2012 when she was referred to me by her Spinal Consultant in a neighbouring hospital. She lives locally to the hospital that I serve but gets specialist care from the hospital with a "Centre of Excellence" status for spinal conditions.

From the outset Kirsty has always been very" down to earth" and has a very practical and positive approach to coping with the difficulties she has. That is good for me because that's the direction that I like to take when considering orthoses that might help to make life a little easier. Oh, by the way, I am an Orthotist!

When we first met she was using bilateral drop foot devises, insoles, knee braces and a spinal jacket.

I listened to her story and looked at how her orthoses were being used and how they fitted. I examined her muscle strengths and range of motions in the joints concerned. We prioritized her main difficulties, at the time, and these appeared to be her unstable knees and her weakness to pull her feet up during walking, so this is where we started. I ordered some different types of knee braces and AFO's to what she was currently using in order to achieve the support she required but in a different way.

In the past eighteen months I've seen Kirsty about eleven times for fittings or reviews, the reviews were sometimes instigated by me and sometimes instigated by Kirsty. We have moved on to consider a different spinal brace, and just now we are changing this again to try and get an optimal brace that helps the most. There are no definitive treatments in orthotics, everybody is different, and each brace has its pro's and con's, it's a case of giving each one a fair trial and trying to work with it before perhaps moving on to another option. Sometimes it comes down to ageing that the present orthoses is the best we can do, there's always a compromise to be made, but we try and keep these as small as possible.

I'm sure that this is just be the start of a long relationship with Kirsty and her Orthotics, and I hope that in the future I can help Kirsty in some small way to achieve her life goals. Her mum, who is also a patient of mine, said I should say how much of a pain she is to me, but I can't say seeing Kirsty in my clinic is "a pain", just time consuming, in a nice way!

By: Steve Shiel
Orthotist

Mary Brennan
My practice nurse

I have known Mary for many years now and we have become very good friends, she understands my phobia of needles and although my veins always riddle and burst Mary manages to do my blood test without having loads of attempts.

Kirsty is a little gem with a kind and caring nature with a smile that makes my heart skip a beat.

I am Kirsty's practice nurse. Kirsty has a needle phobia and comes to see me for injections and blood tests. She always comes to surgery with her lovely mum Julie. Kirsty makes me laugh because when I give her injection or blood test she always stuffs her jumper in her mouth and says nursery rhymes rather than swear.

She is so brave so I reward her with a smiley face plaster and a little hug.. It's a wonder that I can concentrate because she makes me laugh so much.

Kirsty has gone through so much pain but she never fails to give that beautiful smile... God bless you Kirsty and lots of love always.

From your friend and nurse
Mary Brennan
xoxoxoxoxoxox

What some of my friends have to say

Jill, one of my ambulance drivers

I have known Kirsty since 2004. I used to pick up Kirsty and her mum Julie and take them to hospital appointments for Kristy's condition. I worked at that time with the North West Ambulance Service on the non-emergency service. Our job was to collect patients and take them to their hospital appointments. We have recently be taken over by Arriva we are doing the same work as with the North West Ambulance Service.

Kirsty was always a bright funny girl who would give me a hug when she saw me, she has never let her condition get her down, she always has a smile for the ambulance staff, we would chat all the way to the hospital, she would also play tricks on us some of the time.

I knew at times Kirsty was in a lot of pain during

these pick ups but she would never mention it, you just saw it in her face and her mum would have a worried expression. I have so much respect for Kirsty and her family, they amaze me with their strength and courage.

Kirsty does a lot for charity and is always planning new things to do. I have had the honour of attending one of the charity nights with my daughter Melanie and work colleague Tracey and her family; we were all very impressed with how well it went that night.

My daughter Melanie and I have been on a few of Kirsty's Spookathons with her and her family, we have stayed in haunted places overnight they are fun nights but it can be quite scary at times and it helps to raise money for her charity.

Kirsty has grown from a lovely little girl into a beautiful young woman who is now working in television.

Kirsty is an inspiration to everyone who knows her and I was thrilled and so excited when she received her MBE, it was well and truly deserved

I do not collect Kirsty for her hospital appointments anymore as she has her own car so is able to attend her own appointments. I stay in touch with Kirsty and her family and class them as true friends.

Love you loads
Jill Woodworth x

Jill Camps at one of my book signings

Hi everyone,

Now what can I tell you about Kirsty? Well, I could write a book myself at the pranks she has pulled on me when I go on Kirsty's charity ghost nights, which see does for her chosen charity and they are always fantastic. I always end up with a few more grey hairs and not from the ghosts but from Kirsty playing tricks on me.

Joking apart though, ever since I met Kirsty I knew we would be friends as she loves life know matter what is going on she always sees a better side to it if you could have a friend in your life you would want someone like Kirsty.

I know she is in a lot of pain sometimes but she never lets it get her down she is an inspiration to everyone and I think the word of her. Need a hair dye before I go on your next ghost night Kirsty or should that be after your ghost night?

Love

Jill Camp

Two Poems By Mrs. Ball

Mrs. Ball is a lady who started writing to me after reading my story on the Post Pal website. We have been writing to each other for over ten years now.

Mrs. Ball kindly wrote a verse for my first book and when I asked if she would do you one for my second book she very kindly accepted.

Kirsty gets the needle

Kirsty doesn't like injections, has to have some magic cream
To have injections without needles - that is Kirsty's lifelong dream
Lots of aches and pains she suffers, braces on her back and knees,
Good and brave as any soldier - up until the nurse she sees
armed with hypodermic needle marching up to Kirsty's side
Kirsty, when she sees her coming underneath the clothes will hide.
Mum will get the magic cream out, rub it on her arm or thighs,
Nurse has done her worst now Kirsty you can open up your eyes.

....

Friendship

Friendship is to say "hello" to everyone you meet
whether it be a lifelong friend or a stranger in the street,
A "you can ring me anytime" and mean just what you say
and let them know if they need you, you are just a call away.
A listening ear is many times worth more than doctors' pills
To have a friend to talk to isn't the cure for all their ills
but sometimes just to talk it through and get it off their chest,
will make them feel much better and do for them what's best.
They say new friends are silver and old friends are worth gold
But take each on their merit whether they're young or old.
Just remember when you judge them, they are also judging you
So be the kind of friend you want, a kind friend good and true.

....

Verses written By: **Mrs Marlene Ball**

Mr Harry Singleton
(Donates some signed items to me)

Like most men I find it annoying when I have a cold and on the one occasion when I had the flu it was a "crisis" to me.

However Kirsty has battled through an abundance of hospital visits and operations yet she still retains that great love of life and in particular helping others she believes are less fortunate than herself.

She is enthusiastic, courageous, kind, inspirational, modest determined and her single mindedness has resulted in her helping raise a phenomenal amount of money for her chosen Charity "When You Wish Upon A Star" is simply humbling to nearly everyone of us.

Altruism is surely one of the best traits that any human being can have.

I am a great believer that when we help others we somehow help others as well.

I think this very wise Chinese Proverb sums up Kirsty Ashton perfectly: -

"The fragrance of the rose remains on the person who gives it"

I hope you will enjoy this book and I thank Kirsty for being such a wonderful young inspirational lady.

Mr Harry Singleton

Some Fun Times

This is where my last book left off, now my journey continues. I have had so many exciting things happen to me since my last book; hope you enjoy reading what I have been up to. Having NF does not mean you can't have fun too.

14th April 2010:
I celebrated my birthday on the 5th April and I had a really nice time. I received so many cards and gifts, a lot of my cards came from Post Pal. Post Pal send gifts and cards out to poorly children. I have been on the mailing list of Post Pal for many years now, but I am now too old to be a member.

I have been short-listed in the category of Gill Astarita Fundraiser of the Year award and will be going to the awards ceremony in July. Gill Astarita Fundraiser of the year award is for the fundraiser, who in the view of their peers has shown consistent excellence and best practice in achieving high quality fundraising through either their own efforts or their vision and strategy.

29th April 20010:
My friends and I held a 1940's charity night at one of the local pubs, the event went really well and I want to say a big thank you to Alan and Lesley Bates who helped me with the event. The raffle items that I had managed to raise £805.20p so another big thank you goes to everyone who attended the event; it was really nice to see so many people dressed in the 1940's outfits. Titch (my mascot) was a great success with both children and adults. I am sure we will be seeing a lot more of Titch at my charity events.

13th May 2010:
When I arrived home from hospital this afternoon I had a letter that had come for me from Buckingham Palace, when I opened it, inside was an invite to the Queen's Garden Party on the 22nd June for both my mum and me. At first, I could not quite believe that it was true but I filled in my reply slip. I was of course accepting the invitation and would go accompanied by my mum.

The letter states that we must wear a dress and a hat and unfortunately we cannot take any pictures, as they will not let you take your camera in to the grounds of the palace.

I have had lunch with Prince William and Harry and now I get to meet The Queen, how cool is that!

Mrs Julie Ashton

Prince William and Prince Harry
request the pleasure of your company
at a Lunch
on Saturday, 30th June 2007
in the Royal Suite, Wembley Stadium

Pour Mémoire

Time: 12.30 pm
Dress: Informal

My Invite to have lunch with Prince William and Harry

Prince William chats to my mum and me.

*The Lord Chamberlain is
commanded by Her Majesty to invite*

*Miss Kirsty Ashton
and Mrs. Julie Ashton*

*to a Garden Party
at Buckingham Palace
on Tuesday, 22nd June 2010 from 4 to 6 pm*

This card does not admit

Our Invite from Buckingham Palace

28th May 2010:

I have bought my outfit for The Queen's garden party and I even managed to find a hat. The hat that I bought when I was out with my friends last week my mum said would not do and that it looked like I a butcher's hat, 'it just looks like the one that Graham wears on Corrie'. My mum took the hat back for me and bought me a different one. Well, I don't wear hats and it's not every day that you get invited to The Queen's garden party.

Just working on how we are going to get there at the moment as my dad is working and can't take time off work. Looks like it will be on the train, just worried about the sickness on the way, if I am in the car and start being sick it's not so bad, but it's not nice if I start being sick in front of other people and it comes on so quick that I can't just get up and run to the toilet so I have to keep a bowl at the side of me. Only other thing I can do is not to have anything to eat or drink and I will be OK.

10th June 2010:
Today I went along to meet Mrs Kirsty Craig (Daniel Craig's Mum, James Bond) in Chester. This is because not so long ago, I won a business connection award and Santander Community Award. This was for the style of work that I have been doing and the skills I have used are to a business standard. And due to doing a lot of community work I was awarded the Santander Award. I was unable to go to the event on the Friday because I was in Ireland. So I met Kirsty Craig on the Friday. I was happy and honoured to receive both of these awards, and I was happy to receive the £500, which I am going to donate to the charity "When You Wish Upon a Star".

I have now become very good friends with Kirsty Craig and have met up with her a number of times.

Mrs Kirsty Craig hands me my award

23rd June 2010:
Yesterday, I went to The Queen's garden party with my mum, which was a great experience. When I woke up I

was really excited I never slept well all night. When I got up I tried on like six dresses as I had bought so many and five minutes before the photographer from the *Manchester Evening News* came I got changed again. I was then happy with my choice.

When luxury carmaker Bentley heard about me and what I had done for other poorly children they kindly dispatched a chauffeur-driven car to my home to take me all the way to Buckingham Palace and home again.

When the Bentley car and David (my Chauffeur) arrived, I was so excited when I saw how beautiful the Bentley was, I was made up, I was so happy and felt privileged that someone had organised this ride for me. I loved the smooth ride there and back, and it was really comfy. I think I might invest in a Bentley ha, ha. Mum and I turned heads when we arrived at the palace gates in a £130,000 Continental Flying Spur. "It was absolutely amazing".

I was made known and taken through, after the press took several pictures. I went through the Buckingham Palace gates through a check at the main entrance and then taken through the palace and into the palace garden. It's an absolutely huge back garden and it's kept immaculate (as you'd expect). We wandered through the garden before making our way to one of the tea tents for refreshments.

I had some lemon juice and lined up for some posh cucumber sandwiches and cake. The food was lovely and the cakes were lovely too. I enjoyed the iced coffee. I then lined up and waited to see The Queen and The Duke go past. It was a really hot day and even though I never got to say "Hallo" to The Queen or The Duke, just being there and seeing them both walk past was amazing.

Two bands were playing throughout the day and that was awesome and so relaxing. I sat back in the sun hoping to catch a sun tan near the lake and eating an ice cream. My day was amazing and I am so happy I was invited. David my chauffeur was such a nice guy and very friendly and he helped to make my day special too.

The timetable for the day ran as follows:

At 3.00pm the royal gates opened; 3.30pm tea was served in the main tent, which were cucumber sandwiches and ham sandwiches along with some very fancy cakes and iced coffee, tea or juice.

Around 4.00pm the National Anthem was played to announce the arrival of Her Majesty the Queen and members of the Royal Family. The guest to the garden party formed two lanes to allow The Queen and members of the Royal Family to move among the guests, while The Queen was taking tea in the Royal tent. We wandered off towards the lake and sat by it for a while eating an ice cream.

At about 5.50pm The Queen and members of the Royal Family departed and the National Anthem was played again. After everyone clapped the Royal Family we went back to the lake; it was a lovely day and one that both my mum and I will remember for a very long time to come.

I am really grateful to the *Manchester Evening News* for arranging for me to travel by Bentley and to Bentley for agreeing to take me. The whole day was amazing.

David my Chauffeur opens the door for me.

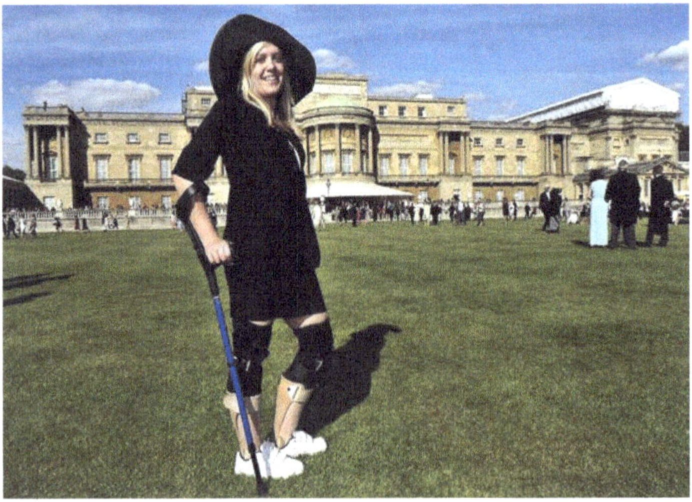

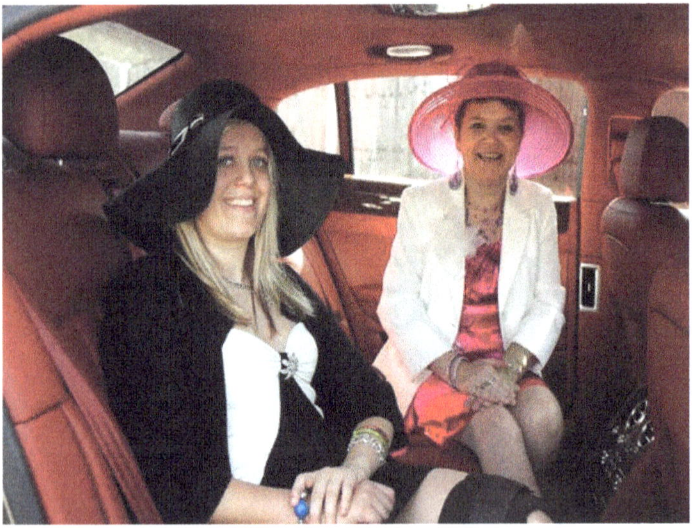

This is one of the pictures taken By the Manchester Evening News

10th July 2010:

I had a great time in London at the fundraising awards and met some lovely people, I was not one of the big winners but it was an achievement getting to the final three.

I went to watch the X Factor auditions today with my mum and one of my friends (Emma), it was a very long day and my mum got to see Simon Cowell, we were only about ten rows back from the front so we were sat in a really good place. I am going again on Sunday as I managed to get some more tickets.

I have not got much else on this next two weeks as I have got a few hospital appointments that involve me having to spend the full day in hospital having test.

19th July 2010:
I went to the M.E.N arena to day to watch the Real Radio Big 15th Birthday Bash. When I got there my friends from the "When You Wish Upon a Star" office greeted me. It's always great to see the girls. We went to McDonalds for some lunch, burgers and drinks. After this we were invited back stage and greeted by a few artist who were performing on stage. I was really excited to meet Scouting for Girls, as I really do like them and think the lead singer is amazing (Roy) they were all really down to earth and lovely. I loved every moment. I also loved meeting the X Factor runners-up and winners; to see how far they have come was great. The singers that I met had photos taken with me and signed my autograph book plus they signed a poster for me that I am going to have framed and then auction it. When we went through to the concert it was awesome as I could see so much and I loved every moment, I was singing along to all the songs and on the boy bands I was dancing away and taking lots of pictures.

1st September- 17th September 2010:
I went on holiday to America with my family, we all had a really nice holiday. We went down to Miami for a couple of days and while we were there, there was a mini hurricane, which I thought was kind of cool. I was happy it was not disruptive and that it did not cause any damage, we just had difficulty standing up as the wind was blowing us off our feet.

While we were in Florida we went to Magic Kingdom and Typhoon Lagoon. When I was in Typhoon Lagoon I went swimming with sharks and I sank as I choked on the water; one of the lifeguards saw that I was in difficulty and saved me.

On the flight home from our holiday and only two hours into the journey I became really poorly and was in a lot of pain in my chest, so I was put on oxygen for the remaining six hours of the flight home. The flight crew kept coming up to me asking if I was OK, the pilot was going to divert the flight so that I could be taken off the flight and taken to hospital, but I was OK to carry on to Manchester Airport. An ambulance met the flight and I was taken into hospital the minute I landed. After spending the rest of the day in hospital I was allowed home later in the evening.

12th November 2010:
The charity Spookathon that I organised went really well and I would like to thank the following people for supporting the event: Craig Gazey (Graham from Corrie), my ambulance drivers, friends and family, The Manchester Paranormal Team, Paul (09 Management), Will Hayes (Candidate 23) and the M.E.N readers for supporting my event.

I have just found out that I am the regional winner for the Spirit Award for all round commitment to volunteering and will now go forward to see if I am to be named the overall winner next year.

I have also received an invitation to the Lord Mayor's Annual Reception on the 25th November; this is a very special event on the civic calendar and something that I am now looking forward to.

16th December 2010:
Candidate23 are a 5-piece Indie Rock Band from the

North West of England, their music has a unique and impressive sound. They are currently playing to audiences across the country. Their first single *One for You* was released on the 24th November 2010 and I was very honoured to be part of the launce party. I also did a collection for my charity; the collection raised £69.73p.

My Spookathon raised £1593.50p with some more money still to come in.

I was at the "When You Wish Upon a Star" office yesterday, as I had to take all the money in that I had raised. I was also doing some filming for the "Spirit Award"; I have now got to attend an award ceremony in March when I will find out if I am the overall winner.

The Lord Mayor's annual reception on the 25th November that I was invited to was really good and I was given the opportunity to meet so many other people who help out in their community.

21st February 2011:
I am really pleased to have my book out and for others to be reading my journey with Neurofibromatosis and Scoliosis. It does feel a little weird though to see my book in print. I have received a lot of good feedback from people who have read my book, some from people who can relate closely to what I have experienced with NF and others who just want to learn more about NF.

The book is just the beginning for me, I have got so much more planed, getting there may be a rough road at times but I'm not going to let NF stop me and together we can help each other.

I am really excited about sharing my story with the world of those living with NF and Scoliosis and I hope by doing so it helps to bring a little hope their way.

15th March 2011:
Yesterday, my mum, brother (Chris), my friend (Daniel) and I went to see Sally Morgan, which was great fun. I gave her a copy of my book and my mum bought me a copy of Sally's book. Sally put my book on her web site, which was really nice of her.

17th March 2011:
My mum and I were invited to London for the V inspired awards. The venue was being held at the indigo2 at the O2 arena. It was great to meet so many inspiring people and everyone was really nice. Leigh Frances was at the event and in fact it was Leigh who was announcing the spirit award winner.

He was so funny and had the audience in stitches. I could not believe it when Leigh announced that I was the winner. I won a lovely trophy (really heavy) and £1000.00 towards any project that I am doing for charity.

I met so many other young adults who had done amazing things for their community and everyone in the room was a winner to me.

Leigh Frances handing me my award

Leigh Frances starts making me laugh

April 2011:

I had a lovely 21st Birthday, which I spent in Tenerife. I would like to say a big thank you to all my friends and family for all the lovely cards and gifts that I received, I loved each and every one of them.

Charity Band night:

What a great night, everyone enjoyed listening to the different bands at the same time money was being raised for "When You Wish Upon a Star". The event raised £448.00, which I was really pleased with.

The bands, solo singers and DJ all donated their time for free, and Keith printed off my tickets and poster for free. I have a great network of support and I could not do what I do without these guys.

28th October 2011:

This morning I did a radio interview about my book at BBC Radio Manchester with Heather Scott.

I have been very busy over the last few months, not only with hospital visits, but also with university, fundraising, and doing radio interviews about my book.

I recovered well from my last surgery but after my next charity event in December I have got to go back in hospital for more surgery, Mr Christopher Duff is going to do the surgery, he is a really nice guy and very understanding.

I have been away to the USA with my family for two weeks. I am now busy working on my charity spook night. I am staying in Hyde Town Hall again to raise money for the "When You Wish Upon a Star" charity. If it's anything like last time we are all in for a great night. We had so much ghostly activity last time; the event also raised over £1000.00 for my charity so I am hoping to raise even more this time.

I was named in the finals for the Red Cross award at the beginning of this month. I had to go to London and was allowed to take two guest along with me so a couple of my friends came with me; my mum and dad could not come as they were at an NF meeting in Manchester. I was meant to be doing a speech at the NF meeting but due to the awards I could not attend the meeting, but I have promised that I will do my speech at the next meeting that they have. I did not win the Red Cross award but again it was a nice opportunity to meet other young people who do nice things for others.

17th November 2011:
I have been asked to explain what winning the V Inspired National Award last year meant to me, so here goes:

"Being a winner at the V Inspired National Awards last year was a really big honour, and going to the awards in London was an absolutely amazing experience. There's such a negative attitude towards young people, so it was brilliant to be part of an event that shows all the good things we have to offer. If you know a really inspiring young volunteer please nominate them now. I'd love to see another volunteers from Manchester get to the finals!" Do you know a young volunteer doing great things in their community? Someone who is always helping others or working tirelessly to change things for the better?

My book is still selling well both in the UK and USA. My book sold out in WH Smiths in the Trafford Centre in Manchester and they ordered more copies, which was great news as all the royalties are going towards my fundraising target and having a second book published.

8th December 2011:
I have had a busy month at university and will be glad to take a rest over Christmas. I have also been busy getting ready for my charity spook night, which I had last Saturday, over 30 people took part and everyone had a great night, I would like to say a big thank you to the Manchester Paranormal Team who came along and provided their time for free. As well as raising over £450.00 towards the cost of the night, they also put on a buffet – a big thank you to the boy band Candidate23 who came along after they had been doing a gig during the evening, the boys looked tired but still managed to stay the full night.

2012

1st January 2012:
I was unwell Christmas Day and slept most of the day. Santa came to see me, which was great, so I must have been good. I received a Peter Andre Calendar. But the calendar is more or less being used as posters around my bedroom. I would love to meet Peter Andre one day, fingers crossed my wish may come true.

The biggest news that I have to tell you is that I have been named in the New Year's Honours List and I am to receive an M.B.E from The Queen. I am still very much in shock by this news.

On Saturday the 31st December 2011, it was announced publicly in The Queen's New Year's Honours List that I am to receive the M.B.E. Being chosen to receive an M.B.E for the work I have done means so much to me and is very exciting. I feel very honoured. The vast majority of people recognised in the New Year's Honours List include those supporting the Big Society by making a real difference to their local community through volunteering, fundraising, social action and philanthropy.

I was one of three people receiving an honour on the New Year's Honours List that was invited down to London to meet with the press. The two other people being, Dr M Philippou, who was also to receive an M.B.E and who is focused on helping young people move away from gang related crime by giving them an incentive to be 'STARS' (Social, Trustworthy and Responsible) and Christopher Preddie, who receives an O.B.E. Christopher, who had devoted his life to youth work and trying reduce crime. He uses his own personal experience to talk to youth groups and prisoners about crime and the huge impact that it can have on your life.

My dad took us down the night before, as we had to meet with the press really early. Can you believe it when I say we were able to drive into the Downing Street grounds, loads of people were stood outside the gates watching as we drove in and parked up while the police searched our car to make sure we were who we said we were. It was all very exciting, we were then showed where to park our car at the back of 10 Downing Street. We were showed into this large room (Chambers) and given drinks and congratulated by members of staff in the room.

My mum and dad sat behind me and I was told to sit in the middle at the head of this large table with the other two people who had also been invited told to sit either side of me. The door opened and about 30 people from the press came in and sat round the table, they were each given notes as to why we had been given the honours and we were told to say a little bit about the work that we do and at the end they were allowed to ask questions. I was asked to go first, I spoke for about ten minutes just telling them about the charity and why

I felt it was important to me, then it was Dr M Philippou's turn. Dr Philippou was one of old type school teachers and took us back to when she was a young girl at school, and after 35 minutes of her talking they had to ask her to finish, but she still had a lot more to say and carried on for a further 15 minutes. In the end they had to explain that they were running out of time and that Christopher still needed to say why he had received an honour. At this point she did pass over to Christopher who then spoke for about ten minutes. The press asked if I was the youngest person to receive the M.B.E and they were told that I was the youngest person this year. After 15 minutes of answering questions we were each interviewed separately. When I got home I had loads of TV and radio interviews: I was on the ITV main news, local BBC North West News, Granada News, and a few radio interviews as well as being in the press, I even made front page news of the *Manchester Evening News*.

I hope by receiving the M.B.E it will help my charity work as the children that I help really deserve their wishes to be granted, they each spend a lot of time in hospital having painful treatment. I have been one of those children to spend months in hospital, and knowing my wish was going to be granted really helped me. I still attend hospital frequently, I still have to have painful treatment and the older I get it does not get any easier for me, but knowing I can help other poorly children helps me forget about my hospital treatment.

I have not been given the date for when I am to receive my M.B.E yet but have been told I will be given six weeks' notice. I am really excited about it, but I really don't know what I am going to wear.

I have received so many cards of congratulations from people who read my story in the *Manchester Evening News* along with some kind donations and I would like to thank you all.

This is just a few of the cards, letter and fist full of money that I received from the *Manchester Evening News* readers.

My first book is now on kindle, my publisher wanted do it for me but he wanted 50% of the royalties and I am selling the book to raise more money for charity so don't really want to go giving the publisher more money. I am also hoping to start some more work on my second book soon as lots of people have asked if I will do a follow up to what they have read so far.

3rd January 2012:
I am to be a V.I.P at The North Pole Bar, I had entered a competition to see a young man perform called Lloyd Daniels. Lloyd is an amazing singer. He was a

contestant in X Factor in 2009 and got through to the final six. I was gutted when he went, so when I heard about his gig where only 50-100 people could go I had no hesitation in applying. I received a call the day before to say that I had been picked. My mum and I went along to watch Lloyd sing and we sat at the front watching him. At the end of the gig Lloyd took time to talk to all his fans one by one and in a group. I have lots of pictures taken with Lloyd. I got talking to Lloyd and we exchanged phone numbers. I was kind of shocked that Lloyd asked me for my number but I was not going to complain, or say "No".

17th March 2012:
I went round Romiley dressed as Miss Wolley and my mascot "Tich" advertising a sponsored Music Marathon that was being done from 12pm till 12am for the charity "When You Wish Upon a Star". The marathon consisted of bands, soloist and instrumentalist who played for around 15 minutes at a time. It was a great event and lots of money was raised.

March 2012:

If you remember at midnight on the 31st December 2011, it was announced publicly in The Queen's New Years' Honours List that I was to receive the Order Member of the British Empire (M.B.E), which I am still in shock about.

On Thursday 22nd March 2012 my family and I were invited to Buckingham Palace for my investiture and I will try to explain what a wonderful experience my family and I had that day.

As you can imagine, prior to the formal announcement and investiture there were some correspondence with myself and the Central Chancery of the Orders of Knighthood (the body who are responsible for organising the investiture). I had to confirm that I actually wanted the award! Incredibly, I do believe that over the years some people have declined receiving the award.

On the day I was allowed to take three guests with me, which made things easy for me as it meant I could take my mum, Dad and brother Chris. We travelled to London the day before, as we had to be at Buckingham Palace for 10am on the morning of the investiture. My brother travelled down later in the day as he had to go to work, and my dad picked him up from the train station later in the day. Unfortunately, someone had broken into our sheds during the night which delayed us leaving for London. Chris said that he would short it out and told us to get going to London as I was also doing a photo shoot while I was in London.

On the morning we travelled from our hotel to Buckingham Palace by car, my brother drove, arriving at the Palace around 10am. We were allowed to park our car inside the grounds of Buckingham Palace where two police officers asked Chris to get out of the car then they asked us to show our invites and ID before being allowed in. There were lots of people outside and I felt really important being allowed through the gates of the palace.

From start to finish the whole affair was like a slick military operation and there were signs indicating where we, the "recipients", had to go, and other signs indicating where the "guests" should go. The award recipients were escorted into a large room to be briefed, while our guests were taken into a huge ballroom where the investiture was to take place. At about 10.30am we, the investitures, had a briefing from the Senior Military Officer from Lord Chamberlain's office. The briefing explained the investiture process and it was at this time we became aware that The Queen would be carrying out the ceremony. During the briefing we were all told that on entering the ballroom we were to wait for our surnames to be called. That would be the signal to move forward, turn left and then face The Queen who would be on a small elevated dais.

Ladies were told to do a courtesy and gents a neck bow, The Queen would then pin the award on your jacket or in my case, my dress. There would be a short conversation and The Queen would then extend her hand to indicate the end of the conversation. That would be the cue to step back from the dais, courtesy again and then exit the ballroom.

What did The Queen ask me? Well, she asked me what I had done to raise so much money and wished me luck and said "well done". The Queen was really nice and smiled while chatting to me.

After the ceremony we all went outside to a huge courtyard where we had some official photographs taken. I felt like a celebrity and did not want it to end but sadly all good things come to an end, and we were soon back in the car and on our way home reflecting on what had been a memorable morning. I still keep asking myself "why me?" and keep thinking I am going to wake up and it's all been a dream.

Receiving my M.B.E from The Queen at Buckingham Palace.

My brother and me outside Buckingham Palace

Less than 24 hours later I was yet again in the company of The Queen and The duke as I had been invited to have lunch at Manchester Town Hall. I was allowed to take one guest with me so I took my mum. We were sat on the next table to The Queen and she looked lovely in her pink outfit. The Queen was at the Town Hall as part of her Diamond Jubilee tour, marking 60 years of The Queen's reign.

When I arrived back home I had to quickly get changed as I was at a charity night with my friends Emma and Kelly, I did not know it at the time but Kelly had arranged for me to meet Peter Andre who was hosting the charity gala night in Stockport. I started to shake when I was introduced to Peter, he gave me a kiss and chatted with me and I had my picture taken with him. It was filmed for *Peter Andre's Next Chapter*. I had a copy of my book with me so I signed it and gave it to Peter Andre. I also met up with Andy Moss from Hollyoaks who I filmed with when I did Hollyoaks. Andy came up to me and gave me a big hug when he saw me and congratulated me on my M.B.E.

24th March 2012:
I was at the "When You Wish Upon a Star" Ladies Charity Night, where I met some of the Coronation Street cast and Paul Crone (people from the Granada area will know of Paul). Paul came up to me and congratulated me on my M.B.E, he bowed and we chatted, then Paul Sleem came and had a chat. Paul was the DJ for the night and brought me out to the front to tell everyone what I had done and I was given a standing ovation. We did not get home till after 2am, my mum came to the event with me.

I have recently been told that I am to carry the Olympic torch on the 22nd June 2012 in Blackpool, which I am really looking forward too. I will carry the torch for B.M.W.

21st April 2012:
My parents arranged a celebration party at the Hallmark Hotel in Wilmslow, to celebrate my receiving the M.B.E.

I had a lovely evening with all my friends who had come along to help me celebrate. All my doctors came with their wives/husbands and some brought their children; lots of people who had been involved in my medical care who I had become friends with and have supported me over the years. It was lovely to have all my friends in one room. I also had a raffle and raised just under £400.00, which I gave to "When You Wish Upon a Star".

The party kicked off at 7.00pm with a drinks reception, Paul Sleem was my DJ for the night and my friend Lucy Barlow sang some really great songs. I had a hot buffet and later in the evening I had hotdogs served for the guests, with guests departing at 1.00am. My mum and dad had arranged for me to stay at the hotel as I had many friends who had come to my party that were also staying at the hotel as they had travelled from Glasgow and some from Wales. After breakfast we all went back to my house for dinner before heading back home.

30th April 2012:
I was also nominated to go on the Happy list for the *Sunday Independent* and was named on the Happy list. I still don't know who nominated me, but thank you whoever you were.

I am having a big Black and White Ball in October to raise money for "When You Wish Upon a Star" and I have already sold all the tickets, which is good news as we are only in April. I have just got to work on getting items to raffle and auction now.

23rd June 2012:
Yesterday, I had an amazing day from start to finish: I carried the Olympic torch along Fleetwood Road, Blackpool.

My mum and I were picked up at 1pm by Melissa (who works for BMW) and Keith (a police officer) in a BMW and driven to Blackpool.

My brother, Dad and Granddad also travelled to Blackpool so they could watch me carry the torch.

Before I could carry the flame I had to meet all the other people who were carrying the torch. We met at our designated collection point to board the shuttle bus that took us to our allocated starting point. My starting point was Fleetwood Road, near Warren Drive. When I arrived at my drop-off point there were crowds of people cheering. As I waited for the gentleman who was passing the flame on to me, children all wanting a picture taken with me surrounded me.

Carrying the flame was one of the proudest moments of my life. It was unbelievable watching all the children clapping and cheering and hearing the crowds cheering and shouting as I went past, I was surprised so many people turned up with the weather being so bad.

I did struggle to carry the torch and walk the 300 metres, and one of the police officer noticed I was struggling and came and helped me; she linked my arm and held the bottom of the torch to help me. A Chinese man and woman kept running out to me and the police had to grab them three times, pushing them back into the crowed. It was very overwhelming and absolutely amazing, I really enjoyed every minute of my day and being part of history.

I passed the flame on to Bolton fundraiser, Stacy Young, who set up the charity Shades after her brother died from skin cancer. You can watch the video if you go on my web page.

I am off to California to teach some children radio production as part of my placement and I am going to New York to meet with some families from the Neurofoundation. I will feed back to Professor G Evans and Chris De Winters on how my visit went. The Neurofoundation have also asked to see my book so I'm taking a copy over with me.

27th August 2012:
I have really loved my summer break teaching Media in the US, it's been amazing.

While I was at camp I made lots of new friends in (the region of 30). The majority of them if not all, are friends for life. It's wired, as you meet people you don't think you have anything in common with, but when you're all in one place aiming and wanting the same thing, it's amazing how close you become; the people I met became my family. Erica was like a mum to me, although she is not my real mum, she was there for me if I needed her. She was amazing and lovely.

After camp had finished I got the chance to go travelling, and went to see some of my favourite places: Las Vegas, Las Angelia, San Francisco and New York. I have never been to any of these places and it was something I really wanted to do, so decided to go for it.

I was in the medical centre every day having to take my medication and vitamins, I also got bitten several times and I managed to get badly burnt on my leg, which needed treatment, not much though, it just stung when the blister burst.

I have had a lot of back pain and knee pain throughout my trip, but that's nothing new so I just got on with things the best way I could. Some days I was really tired but again I worked through it. Providing everyone was happy and having a good time, I was happy too. I always tell myself "I can do everything and anything I want" it just may take me longer to do something or I have to go round a different way. But that's kind of cool, right, makes me unique.

My Visit to Las Vegas:
Not much to report on in terms of Las Vegas, I did not go out clubbing or do any gambling (before anyone ask), I am a good girl. Well, I did spend $5 on my last day and this was only because my lovely brother (Chris) is about to lose his job and I did not want to see him short of money, so I thought mmmmmm $5 could end up being $5million so I played and won $2.75, not a lot, I did not think it was even worth wiring it along to him so I just went to McDonalds and got a kid's meal. Lol.

Whilst in Las Vegas, my good friend (Peter) and I went to the Grand Canyon. OMG! That was an early start, but it was really good to go with a friend and when we got there the view was unreal. It was like something in a movie or book. We took a tour bus up to the top, well near enough to the top, we got off and decided to go on a trail, but the thunderstorm came and we got drenched. Pete ran off to do some pictures and I sat under a shelter watching the rain bounce down. What made me laugh is Peter had just run in the rain and got soaked to the skin and then decided to take shelter. The problem now was getting back down to the meeting point, as the buses were delayed due to the storm; pleased to say we did make it in time.

My trip California went well, I have had a lot of pain in my back and some other health issues but I tried to find ways to overcome it. I met with the Children's Tumour Foundation at the end of August and met with others families who also have NF and Scoliosis. I hope the support I gave while I was with them helped in some way.

My visit to Los Angeles:
In some ways I loved Los Angeles and in others, I didn't, it was tacky in my eyes. I expected it to be posh, especially for the price I was paying to stay. I saw the Hollywood sign from a distance, it was cool to see and I learned about how the sign had fallen down and that's all that is left of it. I did not see much of the walk of fame only what was outside my hostel. I don't like walking with my head down so I gave this one a miss, but at least I can say I have walked on the walk of fame. I paid several visits to Santa Monica beach; it is so beautiful there it's unreal. I went with some people I met in the hostel I was staying in, they were lovely people and really kind and caring. On my first night they took me out in a limo to show me the area. I met up with my friend Peter who I had been at camp with. It

was nice to see a familiar face; we spent a few days together going to the beach, Hollywood, etc. I moved on to Inglewood – need I say more, this was the worst place ever, it's unreal. But it was where I met the most amazing people ever. I met up with my good friend Amy who came from San Diego to see me, she is so nice and I'm sure we will be friends forever. I met Amy when I was at camp and I helped produce a DVD for her. It's amazing how you can just get talking to someone and become great friends.

My walking crutch broke, which meant a trip to ER, but they were unable to help me, they said I had to buy a tennis ball or find something that can go on the bottom of it (the rubber thing had come off). I'd seen another walking stick for sale at $20 and was considering buying it and then using the end of it on mine, but it would not fit. I decided to make do with a tennis ball.

I met two young men while in Los Angeles who were the most down to earth lads I have ever met; we got talking over a distance glaze and got on really well. It was late at night and I was freezing and when I get this cold my back goes into horrible mode, where it really kills to do anything, I was already drugged up on pain killers, which were not helping. I understand why I was cold though as if it was this temperature in the UK I would be fine but on holiday I'm not. Anyway, one of the lads gave me his jacket to keep me warm and told me to keep hold of it to stay warm (I left my jacket on the plane), I thought that was really nice of him. I needed something to eat as I had not eaten for a while and they took me to the shops to get me something. We became good friends/holiday romance. I told them I was off to San Francisco and they offered to drive me there, I said it's OK I have my flight booked, he said he wanted to come and see me while I was in San Francisco. On the morning of me going I said my goodbyes, had a big cuddle and made sure we had each other's details... but as I said at camp, it's not goodbye, it's I'll see you soon...

My Visit to San Francisco:
Well, hello there fog, how I miss you. The flight was OK. In fact it was epic, it was like flying in first class: touch screen TV, wireless, I had everything I could want minus a usb charger for my phone.

On arriving at San Francisco I stayed at a hotel, which was near the airport, must say this reminded me of being back home (this is because I live near the airport back home). So all day and night I heard planes taking off and landing, which was cool. I also managed to have a proper chat with my mum on Skype, we were talking for about an hour, which was awesome (I missed my mummy). I had lots of problems with my knees, it was lucky that I took all my knee braces with me and thank the Lord I did as the velcro went on two of my braces and would just not fasten so I could not wear them. On one of the other knee braces all the stitching came undone and the pole that was inside the brace kept falling out. I tried sawing it but it did not help so I had to bin them all. I wish I had taken my fourth brace now as both my knees need support and I only have one knee support with me. I was struggling with just the one knee brace.

I had booked into see a concert and after the concert I was moving on to a hostel. It was OK, not the best but providing I had a bed I was not really bothered. Later in the day I received a text from Jonas (the lad that gave me his jacket when I was cold) asking where I was, so I told him and we texted each other for a while.

I went to Yosemite National Park while I was there

and OMG it took my breath away yet again. My tour guide was (Mike) fantastic. I was in a lot of pain and my knees were swollen, luckily there was not much walking involved, which was good. I walked a little bit to see a dried up waterfall, I could not do much more due to the pain in my knees so I went and sat down while I waited for the others. While I was waiting I received a text from Jonas saying he is now in San Francisco and he had signed into the same place as me. I did not reply as I thought he was joking. When I got back to the hostel I had a felt pat on my shoulder followed by a hug. It was Jonas, he was in San Francisco with one of his friends... I was unbelievably happy. We went out to celebrate his birthday (he was 23). I already had a card, which I had made just in case he did decide to come and see me. We spoke for ages and met up with some other people.

I went to the Golden Gate Bridge, it was foggy and the battery went on my camera, so I was a little annoyed but $0.75, that's like 40p to go to the bridge for a 30min ride ha, ha. I told myself I would go back the next day and that's just what I did. The most beautiful wild card day I could have only dreamt of. It was fantastic. The picture I took will definitely be going on a canvas on my wall when I return to the UK. I decided to take my time and walk the bridge so that I could say I walked over it. It took me well over a hour, more towards two hours really but I did it and that was the important thing for me, I kept stopping along the way whilst I got my energy back and took photos. I had taken all my painkillers, which soon started to help. I wanted to go on the beach but it was at the other end so I decided not to go, preferring to sit on the grass and take in the sun instead. Right guys don't laugh, but I somehow managed to burn my forehead, my nose, my eyes and right cheek, everywhere else was white. After having a rest I went to the Fisherman Wharf and Pier 39, had a good look round and took some funny photos. I went back to the hotel as it was Jonas's last day at the hostel and we had arranged to meet later.

My Visit to New York:
On the flight to New York I was given an upgrade and was told it's like First Class, I was at the front of the plane with extra leg room etc. I got free food, coffee and movies, but halfway through my movie it cut off, I was gutted. I got my laptop out and started writing my blog update so that my mum could do the update for me when she had time. I was in a lot of pain during the flight and I had taken all my medication including the ketamine, I was feeling a little spaced out to be honest. I nearly dropped my suitcase on some guys' head as my arm went. Oopsss.

I was super excited as I was meeting up with Children Tumour Foundation while I was in New York and meeting some other families with NF and Scoliosis.

I went on a three-day tour to see Niagara Falls and Washington DC. The sites of Niagara Falls were beautiful, I got drenched though but that was a good thing as I was really hot. I went on the Maid of Mist, which was a great experience. We moved on to a different location. I was happy to have a hotel room with a king-size bed; a nice comfy bed was very much needed after staying in hostels. I nearly had a heart attack though when I established that my wallet had gone missing, I tried not to panic. I thought it's only a wallet, nothing much in it and then I realised I had been to the bank and withdrawn money and that all my cards were in the wallet. I went downstairs at 3am inquiring if it had been handed in, but no luck. I had to be up at 6am to depart at 7am and I am pleased to say someone handed my wallet in.

I met a girl called "Sam", who was staying in the same hotel as me. She was so cool, she had also been working in America teaching at one of the Summer Camp, but she was more NYC based. We spent the last two nights talking to all hours, the TV was Spanish and Chinese and we could not understand it, she shown me all the love letters her boyfriend Dan from back home had sent her while she had been away. He seemed so sweet. This is so scary though; Sam only lives 10 minutes down the road from me by car, back home. I have already made a new friend for life. Our final night consisted of lots of giggles and pranks; we loved the hotel that much, and we even left them a present.

I was so looking forward to going to Washington DC, the last time I there, was a few years back when I won the UK Huggable Bear Award back in 2008 and Mum and I went there. I painted a picture on the school wall, I would have liked to have visited the school if I had had the time.

That was my summer break, and although I found some things difficult due to being in a lot of pain, the trip was very exciting and enjoyable. My job was to teach media to the children, and to be honest, I could not do anything else due to being on the crutches and in the back brace.

3rd November 2012:
My charity Black and White Ball was a huge success. I had over 340 guest and people were not shy at putting their hands in their pocket and the night raised a jaw dropping 60K, which was one of the best charity events to date. Will Mellor, Nikki Sanderson and some of the Holly Oaks cast came along to support the event.

My next big charity night is in December when I will be staying in a haunted place overnight.

21st December 2012:

My charity ghost night went really well. I went in the building and that's when the nerves started. Fellow friends, whom I love for putting themselves through this night, met me. We had a tour of the building and a coffee before splitting into groups. The building was big with lots of history. We had a lot of glass movement in my group and we also had a picture drawn when we were using the planchet (a planchet is a wooden disc on wheels and has a pen going through the middle of it). Overall I was not that scared. I wished something would just happen to scar me, I guess. I would like to give credit to my friend Jill Camps, she was amazing and incredibly brave. I nominated her to stay in the boiler room on her own for 15 minutes, Jill was really scared and probably went through a lot of TenaLadies, lol. But she did it and she raised £100.00 as Paul donated £100.00 to the charity due to Jill doing this, which was lovely of Paul. The night raised over £1000.00.

I have been working hard recently and I was lucky enough to go to the Palace Theatre and help out with the CBeebies Panto and I really enjoyed the experience. I have made so many new friends and I am really enjoying the experience. I do hope that one day I get the chance to shadow on CBeebies Radio. I have been very lucky and I am honoured to be on the BBC Ability Forum. I have been selected by the disabled people throughout the BBC to represent them. I will be representing them with a few other people as well. I have just had my first meeting with them, which was very interesting.

11th January 2013:

Well, it's the start of a new year and a great year I had last year. Being named on the New Year's Honours' list and being awarded the M.B.E. I carried the Olympic torch in Blackpool and landed a job at Children's BBC; the only problem with the job it will come to an end in April, let's hope I can find another job within the BBC.

My brother got engaged to his long term girlfriend (Stacey) on Christmas Day, I want to send my congratulations to them both and looking forward to being told the date of the wedding now.

2013

29th May 2013:

I have had a busy few months with one thing and another, but I thought you might like to hear about my most recent achievement.

I was invited to the Inspiring Women Awards on the 17th May 2013. The award ceremony took place at the Midland Hotel in Manchester, it was a lunchtime event and I went along with my mum, we had to be there for 12.15pm.

I won, Oh my God... I won most Inspiring Young Woman of the year 2013.

Right I'll calm down and tell you all about it. Two weeks before the awards I had a visit from Jacqueline Hughes-Lundy who is the founder of the awards and Tom (Tom was doing the filming). I was told they were filming all three young women who were finalist, but I now know that they didn't and it was just me! I had an interview and photos taken which I thought the other finalists had done too, but it was just me. It all kind of seems obvious now, but I honestly didn't have a clue that I was the winner, so it made the surprise all the more amazing when my name was called, they showed footage of my interview and I was given a standing ovations. They played Peter Andre singing while I was going up to collect my award (I just love him he's such a caring guy). I really was not expecting to win. I was so pleased to have been told I made the final three. I was over the moon when I won. I was presented with a cheque for £1000.00 to help me with any projects that I want to do, a lovely bunch of flowers and a glass trophy. I was interviewed for the *Manchester Evening News*, which went in the paper the following day and interviewed for Manchester Radio. I believe I was also in the *Chaser Life Magazine*, but I did not get to see that article.

I had a busy weekend doing two charity events. I had two Fun Days to raise money for "Children with Tumours".

6th June 2013:
I have had a busy week in work this week, but as normal loving every moment of it, I have been attempting to write poems and stories for the CBeebies radio channel.

The sun has been shining bright and it's been a glorious few days.

A few work colleagues in another department, asked me about going carting with them (racing at 70mph in a go cart) ... as we all know, I love adrenalin and things that are fast pace, so I jumped at the chance. Some could say I was in my element... 13 lads, one girl, lol. Well I was asked where am I expected to end and I said providing I am not last I don't care, and happily enough

I came 12th. "GET IN". I did the trial course several times and I did OK, I did not spin off track or crash once, but once we all got competing I kept spinning off. I think the worse line I had was off the steward ' do you want me to move the pedals closer so you can reach' OUCH! That hurt.

I have a busy month now with different things taking place, for instance Candidate23, the band which are part of 09 management that support me at my parties are performing in Manchester on Saturday, so if I am better I shall be attending. The following week, work are doing a boat party where we all sing on karaoke down the Quays in Salford, and at the weekend we are looking at going to Blackpool together to go up the tower and onto the pleasure beach. Then it's my gran's birthday on the Sunday.

One thing I would like to say now that you have read about all the fun stuff that I get up to is the following:

NF is a life-long condition, and you must learn to live your life, and not let the disorder rule your life. The more you understand the more you will be in control, so be sure to ask questions of your medical professionals. Find someone you trust, and share your feelings, fears and frustrations. The challenges posed by having NF are hard, but they can be overcome and you are not alone. They say a problem shared is a problem halved. You can always email my mum or me and we will both do what we can to help.

I hope one day we can say "We have found a cure for NF, Neurofibromatosis is now history".

Charities that I support

Through helping the following charities I have developed strength, determination and patience to achieve my goals. Fundraising is an important part of my life and if I can help bring a smile to another child then I'm happy.

If you have a happy, healthy child in your home you can understand what a joy it brings to see them smile.

For these brave and courageous children, many of who have undergo more harsh and painful treatments than any adult, could ever imagine, the need to bring some magic into their lives is of paramount importance, not only for them, but for their families who so bravely fight alongside them.

Children with Tumours
Is a new virtual charity helping children who suffer from Neurofibromatosis (NF). This wonderful charity is raising money to send children who suffer from NF on a five-day camp holiday, which will be filled with laughter and joy. Money will also go towards finding a cure for this cruel condition.

To help and support CwT please visit my just giving link, which is a safe and secure site. You can find the link on my web page at **www.kirstysstory.co.uk**

"Thank You".

Children with Tumours (CwT)
(What Chris de Winters, Trustee had to say)

First launched in May 2012 we believe CwT to be the UK's first virtual charity. Everything is done online and we believe this 'no frills' approach is unique.

There are no offices or staff to fund, which means more of the fundraising goes to the cause.

CwT launched with the purpose of 'building confidence and giving hope 'to those with NF by networking across the world through Facebook and Twitter and collaborating with charities in other countries. Sharing experiences and fundraising ideas is one of the major steps CwT initiated with other charities.

It occurred to us that scientific research is shared internationally so that everyone can benefit from its success. Wouldn't it be a good idea to share fundraising ideas to?

The commercial cogs of the charity wheel have made "giving" big business. People give to something they feel empathy and compassion for. It is our hope that, by offering a more worldly approach to our cause, that we may develop conscious awareness.

Every expectant couple is interested in what their children will look like – their genetic makeup. When you look forward to the birth of a child you think of exciting things such as eye colour – it's the fun side.

We want to take a step back considering the complications and their impact so we can help. A staggering one child per day is born in the UK with NF.

Ignorance is not bliss. It leads to intolerance, indifference and even cruelty.

People often ask, 'How can I help?'

It is clear that education and helping people in the general public understand more about NF, will help them accept and support people within the community and society.

Help can be as simple as letting your friends, relatives and colleagues know about it. Companies can create a web link to the charity site. For those who would like to be more active, there are many ways in which you can fundraise and become a part of this growing family. Just look at the website for ideas. Whatever you can do will help to improve the lives of those with NF

Kirsty Ashton M.B.E has been with us from the beginning.

From day one, she was supporting our PR, ideas for our fundraisers and with her joyous nature and good will. Despite living in constant pain with NF she continues to act as a trooper with a smile and lovely personality to go with it. No job is too difficult for our Kirsty and we are so thrilled that she has adopted us, to champion, as a charity she truly believes in.

Launching CWT was a gamble…we had no staff or volunteers to support us!

Since our launch, we have made so many more New Friendships and support is beginning to develop in many more areas…A big THANK YOU to everyone who has helped make our first year happen and continue to help us grow…without your support we cannot achieve all the things we so desperately want to do for our children.

www.childrenwithtumours.org

By: Chris de Winters, Trustee.

When You Wish Upon a Star

When You Wish Upon a Star has been going for over twenty years, and without this charity I wouldn't have been able to do, or get through some of the difficult times I have had.

They have played a big part in my recovery in various ways. So I thank the When You Wish Upon a Star team in Stockport for all they have done for me. Meeting Santa and swimming with Dolphins are unforgettable experiences.

When You Wish Upon a Star provides wishes for as many brave and courageous children as possible. Each day brings requests to meet celebrities, drive a Formula One racing car, and of course every child's dream is to meet Mickey Mouse.

For the parents of a sick child, the need to make this wish come true is of the up most importance. Making their wish come true is a real boost for the sick children and their families. The children have to suffer grueling treatments and long stays in hospital. Being able to look forward to a wonderful treat is sometimes the inspiration needed to keep the whole family going.

To keep wishes coming in for these poorly children, please visit my just giving link, which is a safe and secure site. You can find the link on my web page at **www.kirstysstory.co.uk** "Thank you'.

When You Wish Upon a Star
(What Ruth Jagger, deputy manager had to say):

When You Wish Upon A Star is a small charity whose aim is to grant wishes for children with a life threatening or terminal illness.

We send families on trips to Disneyland to meet Mickey Mouse or swim with dolphins, we organise shopping trips and arrange celebrity meetings.

Every December we charter a plane and take 100 very special children with their parent to meet the real Father Christmas in Lapland. Everyone has a magical time in this winter wonderland and the precious memories we create will never be forgotten.

We try to provide a "spoonful of sugar" to help our children and their family through the difficult "medicine" their illnesses force them to endure.

We give them laughter, smiles and precious memories, as we create their magical wish and we are only able to do this because of the continued support of many kind hearted and generous people.

www.whenyouwishuponastar.org.uk

By: Ruth Jagger, Deputy Manager

Manchester's Children Hospital

The New Children's Hospital Appeal was launched in May 2006 and charitable appeal supporting the new state-of-the-art children's hospital in Central Manchester.
Toys, games and computers are needed for the children who have to stay in hospital. I have spent many months in the children's hospital and have a lot to thank the doctors and nurses for. If you would like to help in some way please visit the following web site for more information.

www.newchildrenshospitalappeal.org.uk "Thank you".

Money raised will provide:

- the latest equipment for treatment and diagnosis
- accommodation to allow families to remain together during their child's stay in hospital
- toy's and games for our children.

THE NEURO FOUNDATION

The Neuro Foundation is a charity dedicated to the provision of support and advice to those affected by the genetic condition Neurofibromatosis. Our vision is to improve the lives of those affected by Neurofibromatosis (NF).

Every day a baby is born in the UK with Neurofibromatosis. There are over 25,000 people in the UK affected by the condition and, as yet, there is no cure. Approximately half of those affected inherited the disorder from a parent, but the other half will have developed it through a new gene mutation.

Through The Neuro Foundation's network of regional Specialist Advisors and a dedicated Helpline, the charity is able to offer help, support and advice to those affected, their families and those concerned with their care. The charity links families and professionals together, supports research into prevention and treatments, as well as raising awareness of the condition and the challenges it presents.

For more information about The Neuro Foundation please contact the following address:

Quayside House
38 High Street
Kingston upon Thames
Surrey
KT1 1HL
United Kingdom
Tel: 020 8439 1234

Website: www.nfauk.org
Facebook: www.facebook.com/NeuroFoundation

The work the charity does is reliant on the support of volunteers and unpaid individuals – meaning the money goes where it should.

My Supporters

My story was in the *Manchester Evening News* after I had won an award for how well I cope with my condition (NF) and for the fundraising I have done for other poorly children, which I really enjoy doing. The M.E.N readers back in September 2006 named me The Pride of Manchester.

I wrote a letter to the M.E.N post bag thanking the M.E.N readers for voting for me and asking if any readers would like to buy a pin badge and if any reader had any unwanted items that I could put in a raffle to raise money. The response was fantastic.

One of the M.E.N readers who contacted me was Mr. Keith Oldfield who came round to my house with a Digi camera worth £300.00 for me to raffle. We sat and chatted for a while and Keith mentioned that he owned a printing business (the Printon Shop, Cheadle) and offered to do all my printing for me for free. Since then my family have become great friends with the Oldfield family and without the help of Keith and his lovely wife Pat I would not have been able to have two of the charity balls that I have had. They really are amazing friends. "Thank You" Keith and Pat for everything you have done for me. Other readers donated a bike, boxing glove signed by Ricky Hatton, many other signed items and gifts along with lots of donations. I have got a lot to thank the *Manchester Evening News* for.

**Pat, Ruth (from Wish upon a Star), Keith and I
handing over a cheque for over £24K**

"Thank you" to the managing editor of the *Manchester Evening News*, Mr Eamonn O'Neal, the M.E.N staff for your continued support, and to the M.E.N readers who have very kindly sent donations to help me reach my target for other poorly children.

Just some of the M.E.N readers who have continued to support me are, Mr E Archer (my adoptive granddad), Mr M Kelly, Mrs Betty Pickard, Mrs Ball, Mr and Mrs Singleton, and all the people that send in anonymous donations.

Mr and Mrs Singleton, thank you for the signed items that you have managed to obtain for me over the years, as you know they have helped to bring in so much needed funds for the poorly children.

The M.E.N readers have all been very supportive towards me and I am very grateful to them all.

Alan, Lesley and Stacey Bates and my brother Chris for helping to organise the 1940s events, they always went down well, and have helped to raise lots of money towards my target for other poorly children.

The Manchester Paranormal team who help me with my charity ghost night, which always brings some excitement.

Not forgetting my mum and dad who are always there to support me too.

Thank you to Mike Lee (Ian Kershaw's neighbour) for designing the front cover of my book.

Last but not least thank you to Mr Daniel Cooke at New Generation Publishing for publishing my book. Mandy Tragner for proofreading my book and Sam Rennie for working a long side me to get my book to the publishing stage.

My Goals in Life

I have written a bucket list of things I want to do, people I want to meet, and places I want to visit. I have managed to tick a few of them off my list.

People I want to meet:

- Peter Andre
- Dynamo (Steven Frayne)
- Seann William Scott
- Simon Cowell (that's for my mum really)
- Richard Branson (so I can get lots of tips off him on to raise money for charity)
- David Walliams
- Danny Young (achieved this but I was very poorly in HDU at the time)
- Ricky Whittle (achieved this but want to see him again)

Places I want to visit:

- New Zealend
- Canada
- Australia (Melbourne & Sydney)
- California (achieved)

Things I want to do in life:

- Have my book published (achieved)
- Play a part in Hollyoaks (achieved)
- Have a large Star Studded Charity Ball (for charity)

- Sky Dive down a building for charity
- Stay overnight in the most haunted place ever for charity
- Ride in a helicopter
- Work on commercial or BBC radio
- Work back stage on a film set
- Travel First Class on a plane
- Be a foster parent
- Work in children's TV

Glossary

Anaesthetic (general)	A drug used to put a patient to sleep during surgery
Anaesthetic (local)	A drug used to numb a part of the body
Anaesthetist	A doctor who specialises in giving patients anaesthetics
Antibiotics	A medication used to treat, and in some cases prevent, bacterial infections
Benign	Describes a non-cancerous tumour or non-life threatening condition

Blood pressure	The top number is your **systolic** blood pressure (the highest pressure when your heart beats and pushes the blood round your body); the bottom one is your **diastolic** blood pressure (the lowest pressure when your heart relaxes between beats)
Bone Scan	A technique to create images of bones on a computer screen or on film. A small amount of radioactive material is injected into a blood vessel and travels through the bloodstream; it collects in the bones and is detected by a scanner.
Boston Brace	A Boston Brace is a very hard jacket, and goes from the top of your chest to the bottom of your hips to support the spine.

Biopsy	To have a small sample of tissue taken to be examined
Café au Lait Spots	Coffee-coloured skin patches which are flat to the skin
Cannula	A small tube, which is inserted into a vein in your arm or the back of your hand, to inject fluid or connected up to a drip.
Colonoscopy	The endoscopic examination of the large bowel and distal part of small bowel with fibre optic camera on a flexible tube.
Consultant	Someone who provides professional or expert advice

CT Scan	CT stands for Computerised Tomography. A type of x-ray that uses a computer to create lots of cross-sectional images.
Dermatologist	A doctor who specialises in the treatment of skin conditions
Dyslexia	Difficulty in learning to read and write despite traditional instruction. It is not due to a lack of intelligence.
ECG **(Electrocardiogram)**	An electrocardiogram is a simple and useful test, which records the rhythm and electrical activity of your heart.
EEG nerve conduction test **(Electroencephalograph)**	A neurological test that uses an electronic monitoring device to measure and record electrical activity in the brain.

Electroencephalogram	Measures the electrical activity of the heart
Emla cream	A numbing cream which helps to ease the pain of needles
Endoscope	A medical device that is a long thin, flexible (or rigid) tube, which has a light and a video camera at the end of it. Images of the inside of the patient's body can be seen on a screen.
ENT Doctor	Consultant specialising in Ear, Nose and Throat disorders.
Foot Drop	Is the inability to lift the foot and toes properly when walking. It is caused by weakness or paralysis of the muscles that lift the foot.

Gabapentin	A drug that is used either alone or alongside other medicines in the treatment of partial seizures, which are types of epilepsy. It can also be used to treat certain types of long-lasting pain caused by damage to nerves. This type of pain is called neuropathic pain and be caused by a number of different diseases.
Gamma Camera	An imaging technique camera are pieces of apparatus which allow radiologists to carry out 'scintigraphy scans', tests which provide detailed diagnoses about the functioning of the thyroid, the heart, the lungs and many other parts of the body.
Genes	Carry the codes ACGT. We have thousands of genes. They are like our computer program and make each one of us what we are.

Genetic	Refers to the person's strands of DNA, which are configured to form "Genes", which the cells use as instructions on how to function or grow. Genes represent the basic blueprint of our bodies and can vary greatly from person to person.
Geneticist	Scientists, who study genetics, (study of genes) their functions, and their effects.
HDU	"High Dependency Unit": a ward for people who need more intensive observation, treatment and nursing care than is possible in a general ward.
ICU	"Intensive Care Unit": a ward where patients are placed when they need a higher level of care, including closer observation and intensive monitoring.

Ketamine	This drug is used to treat types of pain that conventional painkillers are not relieving. It can be used by itself or in combination with other painkillers to improve you pain relief.
Lung Function Test	Also called pulmonary function tests, measure how well your lungs work. These tests are used to look for the cause of breathing problems, such as shortness of breath.
Morphine	Morphine is used to treat severe pain. It acts on certain parts of the brain to give you pain relief.
MRI Scan	Magnetic resonance imaging is a type of scan used to diagnose health conditions that affect organs, tissue and bone.

Mutation	Mutation occurs when a DNA gene is damaged or changed in such a way as to alter the genetic message carried by that gene.
Nerves	The nervous system is a complex network of nerves and cells that carry messages to and from the brain and spinal cord to various parts of the body.
Nerve Conduction Test	Measures how well and how fast the nerves can send electrical signals. Nerves control the muscles in the body with electrical signals called impulses. These impulses make the muscles react in specific ways. Nerve and muscle problems cause the muscles to react in abnormal ways.

Neurofibromatosis Type 1	A genetic condition that can cause a variety of symptoms, including: tumours that grow along the nerves in any part of the body. They may grow under the skin, or they may protrude from the skin, multiple flat, light-brown patches of skin pigment, called café-au-lait marks. NF1 can cause a myriad of potential complications.
Neurofibromatosis Type 2	(NF2) is the least common type of neurofibromatosis, occurring in about 1 in 25,000 people. Despite sharing the same name, the two types of NF are separate conditions that have different causes and symptoms.
Neurosurgeon	A doctor who specialises in the brain and spinal cord.
Occupational Therapist	Someone trained to help people manage their daily routine, e.g. dressing, cooking and getting around.

Oncologist	A doctor who is qualified in treating cancer.
Orthopaedic Doctor	A surgeon or doctor who specialises in the treatment of bone and skeleton related problems.
Paediatrician	A doctor who specialises in treating children.
Paralysis	A term used to describe the loss of the ability to move muscles, e.g. arms and legs.
PET Scan	A PET scan is a way to find cancer in the body. The patient is given radioactive glucose (sugar) through a vein. The scanner then tracks the glucose in the body.
Physiotherapist	Someone who specialises in the treatment that uses physical movement and exercise to relieve stiffness after surgery or injury.

Plexiform Tumours	Plexiform neurofibromas are extensive nerve sheath tumors that can become quite large in size.
Psychiatrist	Psychiatrists deal with mental health.
Pulmonary Embolism	A blood clot in the pulmonary artery, which is the blood vessel that transports blood from the heart to the lungs.
Radiographer	Someone who takes x-rays
Reflexes	An involuntary or automatic, action that your body does in response to something — without you even having to think about it.
Scoliosis	A condition, which causes the spine to curve

Spinal Cord	A column of nervous tissues in the spinal column that sends messages between the brain and the rest of your body.
Temperature (Thermometer)	Your body temperature can be measured in many locations on your body. The mouth, ear, armpit, and rectum are the most commonly used places. Temperature can also be measured on your forehead.
Thrombosis	A formation of a blood clot inside a blood vessel, which is obstructing the flow of blood.
Tumour	An abnormal swelling on or in the body can be called a tumour. They can be either benign or malignant.
Ultrasound Scan	A way of producing pictures of inside of the body using sound waves.

VG Scan Ventilation Perfusion Scan	Most commonly done in order to check for the presence of a blood clot or abnormal flow inside the lung.
Vitamin D	Vitamin D is important for good health, growth and strong bones. A lack of vitamin D is very common in people who suffer from NF.
V-Tens Machine	A highly sophisticated TENS machine with electro-acupuncture capability.
Whiplash	When muscles, ligaments and tendons in the neck have stretched and strained, often caused by a sudden jerk or jolt to the body.
X-ray	A safe and painless procedure often used to produce images of the inside of the body.

Acknowledgements

I hope you have enjoyed reading my story and that it has helped to give you a better understanding of how a person can be affected by Neurofibromatosis (NF).

There are so many people I have to thank, if you are not mentioned please don't think I'm not grateful to you, I am.

To all the doctors and nurses who have cared for me over the past 23 years, especially Mr Neil Oxborrow, Dr Watts,
Mr Christopher Duff, Dr Smyrniou, Dr Sue Huson, and Mr Thorn. Thank you to Mrs Mary Brennan (who is my nurse at the doctor's) and the nurses at Wythenshawe Hospital and Manchester's Children's Hospital.

To all my family and friends, especially Julie Hesmondhalgh, Ian Kershaw and Ricky Whittle, you have helped me so much through some difficult times. Thank you for always being there for me and supporting me at my events.

My good friends: Keith, Pat and Alex Oldfield. You stuck by me when it really mattered and without your help I would never have achieved my goal in helping other poorly children. You understood how important it was to me to raise money so that wishes could be granted for other poorly children and I'll never forget you for that.

Thank you to my Ronnie Gran (mum's mum), to my gran and granddad (dad's mum and dad), I love you all.

Finally, and most importantly, to Mum, Dad and Chris (brother); you are what keeps me going, keeps me laughing and looking forward to another day. I love you all.

I am here as a support for you, to be a friend, someone you can sound off to when you're feeling down. Anyone can tell you it won't hurt tomorrow, but I'm here to listen when it hurts today.

Lot of love

Kirsty Ashton M.B.E xxx

www.kirstysstory.co.uk
Twitter @kirstysstory

Some reviews from my first book:

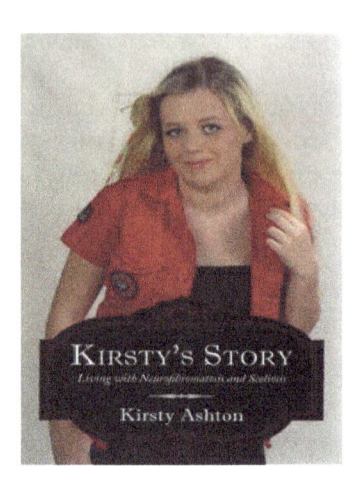

Kirsty's Story Living with Neurofibromatosis and Scoliosis

I really enjoyed reading Kirsty's book (Kirsty's Story living with Neurofibromatosis and Scoliosis). It came from her heart and soul.

I am privileged to be Kirsty's practice nurse at the surgery she attends and she is always such a pleasure to deal with. She never fails to smile that beautiful smile even if she is in pain.

I am also privileged to know Kirsty's family who are a great support to her.

Kirsty has worked so hard with her chosen charity and has raised thousands of pounds…well done my lovely friend and also for being awarded an MBE.

Keep up the hard work and I wish you well for the future, with fondest love,
By: Mary Brennan xoxoxoxoxox
****

Kirsty's Story: Living with Neurofibromatosis and Scoliosis Read this book in one day. Could not put it down. Would recommend this to anyone either suffering NF or not. Having the same condition meant I could relate to some of the things Kirsty went through. Cannot wait to read it again!!!
By: xEmCx

****

Excellent Book

I love the format of the book (journal style) and that Kirsty takes the time to explain the medical terms for the readers who don't know what they mean.

Love the fact that despite all the not-so-good moments, she kept (and keeps) a smile and a positive mind (it surely helps us and the persons around us); and that she decided to pay it forward by helping others.

It feels good to know that I am not alone, and that though they may have it worse than me, they don't give up on hope, which renews my hopes.

Kirsty tells us what she has been through, good and not so pretty, I just wish I could hug her and thank her for being so brave and for the help she gives to others.

The book has a very few typos, but they didn't bother me at all as the content of the book is as beautiful as it can be.

I read the book in two days (yes, I couldn't put it down), and I'll be surely sharing the book with my relatives.

By: DeanNGina

****

Inspirational read and very informative, Ms D Smith

Kirsty's Story Living with Neurofibromatosis and Scoliosis (Kindle Edition)

I read this inspirational and very informative book when my daughter, Katie, was diagnosed with NF1 and scoliosis, just like Kirsty. The book was easy to read and I was able to read sections out to Katie so she gained a good understanding of many of the issues that Kirsty has faced that Katie is/will face – surgery, wearing a back brace etc. It was also really useful and informative having all the photos. The charity work that Kirsty is involved in is so moving and inspiring.

Kirsty's book is a great read for anyone wanting to learn about NF1 and/or scoliosis and its invaluable as a reference book.

By: Ms D Smith

****

Amazing Young Women

Kirsty's Story Living with Neurofibromatosis and Scoliosis (Kindle Edition)

Great book; an inspiration to all sufferers of NF, very brave supportive, informative book. True story of a girl's life with NF and all her medical history through this genetic disorder.

By: Classy Lady

****

Kirsty's Story, Mary Lou
Kirsty's Story Living with Neurofibromatosis and Scoliosis (Kindle Edition)

This is a moving and interesting story of a brave young girl called Kirsty who suffers with neurofibromatosis and scoliosis. I thoroughly enjoyed reading the book and would recommend it to anyone who has feelings and respect for others. Kirsty works amazingly hard for a charity called 'When You Wish Upon a Star' and has raised thousands of pounds... she is now the ambassador for this charity. I am privileged to know Kirsty and her family personally and would like to say how proud I am of Kirsty and also to her lovely family for supporting her. Love you Kirsty :) xxxx

From. Mary Brennan xxxx

****

Kirsty's story living with Neurofibromatosis and Scoliosis

This was a very interesting story of a young girl's journey living with Neurofibromatosis and Scoliosis. Really enjoyed reading what the doctors involved in Kirsty's care had to say too. The book also included lots of helpful information. Kirsty is a true star, thank you for sharing your journey with the world.

By: Jay

****

Kirsty's Story: Living with Neurofibromatosis and Scoliosis,
This great book about a young girl that lives her life to the full and at the same time helps others live their dream.
By: Springwater

****

Very Informative read.
A fascinating true story of a courageous and vivacious young lady.

Someone who is determined to help others less fortunate and to raise funds for the awareness of NF that she herself, has. Three stages of her life are mentioned: Reflection as a child, present life and what Kirsty still plans to do.

The support and love of her close-knit family touches one's soul. Her book motivates one to look beyond your own circumstances and to reach out to others.

You cannot help but fall in love with this exuberant young lady.

Kirsty, you are an overcomer in every sense. Always stay true to the remarkable young woman God created you to be.
By Michelle Bleske Bouwer

****